FINANCIAL TIMES
MANAGEMENT

Knowledge   Skills   Understanding

Financial Times Management is a new business created to deliver the knowledge, skills and understanding that will enable students, managers and organisations to achieve their ambitions, whatever their needs, wherever they are.

Financial Times Pitman Publishing, part of Financial Times Management, is the leading publisher of books for practitioners and students in business and finance, bringing cutting-edge thinking and best practice to a global market.

To find out more about Financial Times Management and Financial Times Pitman Publishing, visit our website at:

www.ftmanagement.com

Part 3
SALES AND MARKETING PROGRAMMES

FOREWORD

by The Rt. Hon. Lord Young of Graffham

Exporting is fun, one British Prime Minister famously said, and immediately all the exporters in the land knew that he had not the faintest idea of the life exporters actually led. As Terry Patrick points out in this book, if you are content to stay at hotels that you would never subject your family to, fly on planes (as I have done) tied up with string, land on airfields that are literally that, then exporting might be for you. Whether it is for your company, this book will help you decide.

But before we get to the reason why the reader should export at all, we should look at the long and distinguished history of exporting in these islands. In the days of Rome, it was wines from Britain that were prized above all. We became a seafaring nation and the ports of Bristol, Liverpool and London quickly paid tribute to our success. When we lost our Empire in the West we quickly set about creating another in the East. Our Navy was there to protect our trade routes. The East India Company laid the foundation for India and whether trade followed the flag or the other way round, we became the greatest trading nation on earth. All the time it was our access to markets, both for exporting finished goods and importing raw materials, that made the difference and was the foundation for our wealth creation with the coming of the Industrial age.

The first beginnings of the Information age was the telegraph and it was no coincidence that the first successful transatlantic cable was laid by Isambard Kingdom Brunel's Great Britain in 1866, driven by the need of the Manchester promoter to have up-to-date market information about the price of Virginia cotton. Four years later and both shores of South America were covered, four years after that India, then in the next few years China, Japan and even Australia. All telegraph cables led to London, for London, particularly the City of London, was the centre of the world's importing and exporting businesses.

Our major opportunities today lie both in the near exporting markets – the European Union – as well as markets further afield. Whether or not we enter the Euro, our European partners are export opportunities. It will take decades for them to really become our home market and the same precautions that we have to take for markets further afield will have to be taken for them.

I would recommend every businessperson to read the first few chapters of this book and work through the questionnaires they contain. At the end of that you might or might not still want to export, but I am certain that you will know more about your own business, and you will benefit mightily. I hope that after that you will decide that exporting is for you and you will go on to construct the business plan and the export financial plan that the author outlines. This is no mean effort, but again, at the end, you will have the confidence that your endeavours have a reasonable chance of success.

For exporting is worthwhile for the company with the right products and a secure home base. Exporting is not a prescription for making up any shortfall in your home sales, nor is it a way of getting rid of unsaleable stock. One way to disaster is to assume that you can export goods or services that are not up to UK standards in either design or quality. First, if the design is not good enough then your chance of sales is greatly diminished, but even worse, if the quality is sub-standard then the cost of returns or repairs will dwarf any margin you have left.

There are enormous opportunities waiting overseas, but like everything in life, success will depend on the amount of time and effort invested in preparation. No potential exporter who reads Terry Patrick's book through from cover to cover, and works through the questions will ever be able to say that they were not warned should matters not work out as planned. On the other hand the exporter who does his or her homework, decides that there is a market opportunity and makes the right preparation in the new market has a much greater chance of success. I wish the reader of this book and indeed, every exporter, well and look forward to meeting them in the months and years to come as we trail around the airports of the world finding out why our flights are, once more, delayed.

The Rt. Hon. Lord Young of Graffham
25 March 1998

ACKNOWLEDGEMENTS

I would like to take this opportunity to thank the many organisations and individuals in over eighty countries world-wide, who have kindly given much of their time and experience to assist me in the research for this book, and especially to Lord Young who most graciously agreed to write the foreword for *Cracking International Markets* at a time when I was six thousand miles away in Siberia and communications were extremely difficult.

My very special thanks go to Graham Mason – life-long friend, stalwart companion, and Director of Eurogistics Limited – without whose encouragement, support and continued friendship in the face of many adversities, this book would never have been completed.

I must also thank the Commercial Department staff at the many British Embassies throughout the world who have uncomplainingly rendered me considerable 'in-country' practical help and assistance over the last twenty years. Special thanks must also go to Mr Mark Date (Head of Visa Section, British Embassy Moscow), who gave much of his time and his staff's effort in assisting to resolve my family visa problems while I was resident in the Federation of Russia.

In addition to the above, my very sincere thanks to all of the staff at Financial Times Pitman Publishing in London, in particular Pradeep Jethi, Iain Campbell, Amelia Lakin, Elizabeth Truran and Elie Ball, who have patiently and efficiently overcome all of the communication problems associated with a 'long-haul' author's manuscript. A very professional team, and a most excellent example of 'Britain at its Best' in international markets.

Finally, I would like to thank my wonderful Russian wife Asya for her total commitment, love and support to me over three long, hard and very cold Russian winters while writing and editing this book, and for the many sacrifices which she has made so that I was able to finally complete *Cracking International Markets*.

My most sincere thanks to you all. May your god go with you.

Terry Patrick
Moscow, Federation of Russia

INTRODUCTION

This book makes no apologies for being closely focused on achieving export sales. If you are currently active in export markets you will know how difficult it is to achieve good sales success in overseas markets, and to develop and maintain consistently profitable and progressive market penetration. If, however, you are a newcomer to exporting, there are many pitfalls to be avoided, and new disciplines to be learnt before you will be able to make your mark on international markets.

There are many different methods, programmes and techniques available for commencing an export programme, each with its own cost overhead, level of complexity, implementation time scales and special resource requirements. However, regardless of the size of an export programme or the complexity of approach, there are a number of common factors.

> Any export market entry – regardless of product, market sector or geographic region – requires professional export market entry preparation and a co-ordinated and comprehensive implementation programme.

Any export market entry – regardless of product, market sector or geographic region – requires professional export market entry preparation and a co-ordinated and comprehensive implementation programme. This book provides much information about how to break into new export markets and a proven methodology for export business development.

POTENTIAL MARKETS

The world is a 24-hour market-place. As the sun sets in London, Los Angeles, Bombay or Melbourne, it is rising on a new business day in other parts of the globe. People are at their offices doing business, selling products, goods and services, and hoping to make good profits! This is your potential market!

For the vast majority of non-exporters, the capital tied up in plant or machinery, office and/or factory premises, semi-finished goods and raw materials is productive for only an average of eight hours of business each day, and for only five days per week. If their business ran for a full 24 hours each day, six or even seven days a week, if they had a professional sales team selling their goods to prospective customers around the clock, this could have a significant impact on profitability. This is the reality of exporting – a global business, 24 hrs per day.

WHY EXPORT?

Too many companies attempt to enter new export markets with no real understanding or evaluation of why they should export. Some companies begin exporting almost by accident. Perhaps they receive a product enquiry from abroad for the first time, and suddenly they find that they are in the export business! Perhaps a member of staff attends an 'International Trade Day' at a local Chamber of Commerce and is

> **Exporting – a global business.**

impressed by the thought of 'wider markets'. Or perhaps the company receives, from their government's export promotion department, brochures describing the business opportunities that exist in foreign markets. A significant percentage of companies, some of which are now recognized leaders in their chosen international market sectors, moved into exporting almost casually, in a relatively unstructured fashion.

The overall rate of failure of 'self-planned' export market entry is far higher than for an 'instant' export order, 'casual' export market entry. An export enquiry, successfully responded to, and of course fully paid for, has demanded that someone in an organization has been very careful to ensure that they achieved a good result. A good initial result, regardless of how 'unplanned', promotes a strong interest in generating further export sales.

However, as has been extensively reported by the media, the failure rate for export market entry is (in the short to medium term of two to three years) very high. Both established multinationals and smaller companies, which have failed to secure and consolidate a new export market, have suffered considerable financial losses. Such failures have often been the result of a belief that an early sales success will continue, but without undertaking a long and often time-consuming export market entry evaluation programme.

One lesson that may be learnt from the failures of others relates to the costs which may be incurred in an export programme. As the operating and overhead costs are usually substantially higher in export markets than in home markets, losses incurred overseas can seriously damage profits generated in the home market. It is therefore vital to separate the company's home and export market accounts, with regular, accurate financial reconciliation and consolidation.

In many organizations the introduction of an export strategy has developed through encouragement and promotion by the marketing department. Although it has not been unknown for an enthusiastic marketing manager to recognize an export strategy as a vehicle for the realization of his or her personal international travel ambitions, in most companies a professional marketing department plays a vital role in identifying export potential. To their credit, most internal export departments usually do a good job of potential export market qualification. However, they often lack staff with practical experience of export market entry planning, and export programme implementation, with which to carry through a new market entry export programme to a successful conclusion.

Having reviewed some of the preliminary factors relating to export market entry, we return to the primary question: 'Why Export?' There are a number of very good reasons why a company should consider an export programme as part of its corporate development. These are presented in the form of a checklist .

Why export?

1 **The current or near forward projected home market is in recession, or moving towards an identifiable downturn in trading conditions.** ☐

2 **Direct competition in your home market is now beginning to have a severe impact on your sales volumes and overall profitability.** ☐

3 **You have made excellent profits (or projected profits) in this financial year, and require a tax liability offset programme.** ☐

4 **You have new products which for some special reason are not readily saleable in your home market, and/or you would like to trial some new products overseas, in order to establish product viability in a foreign market, without impacting home market credibility.** ☐

5 **You enjoy market domination in your current home market, and you cannot expand any further without expensive diversification or acquisition.** ☐

6 **You need to even out quarterly trading fluctuations or seasonal variations in your home market.** ☐

7 **You need to develop additional complementary markets for your current product range, which is already identifiably oversubscribed in your home market.** ☐

Any company considering exporting should also bear in mind the costs involved.

1 There is a considerable financial overhead. Furthermore, new export market entry is not easy, and takes considerable time and resources. A company must be sure that it can afford both the venture finance and the possible distraction from the control and development of its core business.

2 Management and staff will have to acquire new skills, or skilled new staff will have to be recruited and appointed.

Any company considering exporting should also bear in mind the costs involved.

3 A considerable amount of 'dedicated' senior and executive management time will also have to be allocated to the export market entry programme, as many of the decisions required cannot be delegated to junior staff.

If, as in most companies, it is the possibility of additional profit generation that attracts you to exporting, you should consider the following additional profit generation possibilities in your home country before finally committing your company to an export programme.

Home country profit generation

1 **Invest in a professionally produced advertising promotion or sales drive in your current home market to secure additional sales.** ☐

2 **Undertake a major cost reduction exercise in all areas of your home market operations to reduce operating costs and to enhance the overall financial performance of the company.** ☐

3 **Undertake a comprehensive stock review to try to reduce your investment in stock and raw materials.** ☐

4 **Explore all methods of persuading your customers to pay you more quickly to improve cash flow.** ☐

5 **Consider investing in a new product development programme to put pressure on competition, and increase your market share in your home market.** ☐

6 **Implement a special sales commission, bonus or incentive scheme to further motivate sales staff to achieve additional sales.** ☐

7 **Consider or investigate factoring your invoices.** ☐

8 **Consider consulting a professional 'Company Doctor' to give an independent overview of your company's current performance and evaluate future potentials.** ☐

9 **Hold a major, well-advertised sale to dispose of old, unfashionable or technically outdated stock.** ☐

If you have not considered all the possibilities in the checklist, and your reason for entering new export markets is mainly profit generation you should undertake a thorough review of the additional options for improving your current home market profit performance first.

We now move on to consider the construction of a professional export market entry programme.

Entering a new export market requires detailed planning and the designing and implementation of a comprehensive and detailed export plan. The old adage, 'Failing to plan is planning for failure' is particularly relevant here. The pioneering spirit and enthusiasm of sales staff to obtain business may need to be contained in the early stages of an export sales programme. As well as detailed planning, substantial pre-entry market research will greatly reduce the business risk and the inherent financial exposure factors associated with exporting. Each part of the planning process is self-contained, but totally dependent on the other parts for its overall success.

> **This book brings together the basic components for developing a world-class export market entry programme.**

HOW TO GET THE MOST FROM THIS BOOK

This book brings together the basic components for developing a world-class export market entry programme. It offers a comprehensive and detailed methodology for finding solutions to exporting problems and dilemmas. Some of these solutions may not be required in every export market entry programme, as the approaches required for individual products and market sectors vary from company to company, and from product to product.

This book is arranged in three parts covering the entire process of entering export markets.

- **Part 1** looks at market entry, and leads you through the steps you need to take as you prepare for entry. It includes an executive briefing on exporting; a 'company fitness programme' for evaluating a company's skills for exporting; training requirements; and preparing to devise an export plan.

- **Part 2** sets out the detailed requirements for creating and refining an export business plan and an export financial plan. It looks at every aspect of these vital processes. It includes the recording of information about your product and its market; consideration of the business mission statement; qualifying and confirming export market potential; financial procedures; market research and opportunity analysis.

- **Part 3** examines sales and marketing programmes. It looks at the question of sales quotas and targets and compares the different sales methods – agents, distributors, direct representation and other options.

Each part of the book is structured to include key points, checklists and reviews, as well as practical examples and real-life case studies drawn from a variety of market sectors. A prudent approach to an export programme demands that you complete the detailed checklists throughout the book before implementing each successive part of the programme.

A final point before we close this introduction. Some aspects of exporting procedures involve detailed technical and legal documentation – particularly those associated with export documentation, hazardous goods, import/export regulations and controls and international contracts. These are all very specialized subjects, often complex in format and quite often subject to a degree of interpretation. You are strongly recommended to seek the advice of a recognized expert in such matters before commencing any physical exportation of your products or services.

Part 1

MARKET ENTRY

Chapter

1

WHY EXPORT?

INTRODUCTION

Second only to seeing your first product roll off your brand new production line, and the realization of your dreams when your product or service offering has been sold to your very first customer, is perhaps the satisfaction of securing your first export order in a brand new overseas market. Both of these situations are milestones in the development of a company, and will always remain special memories in the hearts of all true business entrepreneurs.

If you are an owner, a founding director, or a senior executive manager of a company, you have a special and vested interest in the successful outcome of the new business. You will almost certainly have had to work long hours, often completely on your own, to overcome all the development problems associated with the start-up of the company – and with setting up and implementing all of the administrative and business management routines. You will have had to come to terms with all of the implications, problems and difficulties of professionally managing your cash flow, production, stock, logistics, finance and accounts receivable.

By your choice and selection of this book (unless you are already established in an export market and have found that it is somewhat more difficult than you envisioned), you are now almost certainly at a stage in your company's development where you are reasonably well established in your home market, and are looking for additional ways in which to expand your business. Exporting is the next logical step forward for companies whose products and services are suited to international environments, and who wish to expand their sales into additional markets.

So, we come back to the fundamental question 'Why Export?' The answer is relatively easy. If you truly believe in profit as the prime business objective, and if you have exhausted all the profit potentials of your home market through professional sales and business management programmes, or if you are in a situation of diminishing returns for capital employed, then, and only then, should you turn your attention to exporting.

DEVELOPING THE HOME MARKET

There is one thing for certain: it will cost you a great deal more to establish good sales volumes in new export markets, than it will for you to achieve similar results in your home market, all reasonable factors being equal. So, please review the APGs (Additional Profit Generators) carefully and select and implement the appropriate actions for developing your home market before you implement an export programme. This gives you the best possible base from which to develop your new export business programme.

The above statement in no way precludes you from entering into the initial phase of exporting – export market research – or prevents you from commencing all the necessary review programmes you must undertake to prepare your company for exporting.

A company often can find it very instructive to undertake a home market profit enhancement/optimization programme which has no direct bearing or implication on their export objectives. As the Prussian general Clausewitz wrote, in his classic military handbook, *Principles of Modern Warfare*, the very first principle for winning a battle is: 'First secure the home base'.

By commencing your export programme with an in-depth company review and profit enhancement programme, you will also protect, reinforce and secure your home company base, and even if you are not as successful as you would wish to be in your new export venture, you will still have a good, viable and profitable business in your home market to fall back upon.

It is vital that you always bear in mind that a poorly executed 'high cost' export programme can seriously impact your home market profits and could place your core home market business at risk. When making important, particularly strategic decisions relating to your export programme, always preface the decision-making process with: 'What profit impact will this export decision have on my core home market business?'

There are thousands of companies, including a very significant number of famous multinationals, who in hindsight recognize the wisdom of this statement. The smaller your business, the greater is the risk of home market profit impact, as few small to medium sized companies have the financial reserves to 'write off' substantial overseas losses without major cash flow implications. This potentially very serious impact is covered in greater detail in Chapter 11 Remember – pre-warned is pre-armed! If a major part of your export project is recognized as being dubious or fragile in terms of profit realization – discontinue the project. This will take courage, but it is the safest route.

A PROFESSIONAL ATTITUDE

We now turn to all the issues, plans and programmes which will ensure professional, cost-effective and profitable export market entry. The first issue we need to address is the question of attitude.

Exporting is a very serious potential part of your business. It is also exciting, stimulating and often frustrating, but very worthwhile if tackled in the right manner. A positive professional manner and attitude are essential. Exporting is not for the fainthearted, semi-committed or negative. It requires boldness, confidence and dedicated professionalism to achieve success.

You should remember that, unless you have a very special product or service, or you are in an extremely specialized niche market, almost any product, with only a few exceptions, can be sold in any of the major markets throughout the world – provided that the cost-benefit ratios are acceptable to the buyer!

INFORMATION GATHERING AND DEVELOPING A DATABASE

Information gathering

The first exporting activity to be addressed is the information gathering exercise.

At the beginning you will not have definitive information about where your best markets are, or which products or services you should offer as 'lead products' in those markets. You may have some ideas, but this question requires detailed clarification and qualification prior to investment commitment.

In order to get the best value from the initial information gathering stage, acquire information on as broad a base as possible. If you are totally new to any form of export business, start with a visit to your local reference library. Here, you will find a good selection of information on exporting, export procedures, overseas markets and books with lists of contacts to help you. There should also be a list of all the central government departments concerned with exporting and overseas trade. In addition, most countries have organizations such as chambers of commerce, trade associations and exporters associations which provide other useful information.

Evaluating market opportunities

Read as much as you can about your potential markets to begin with. Try to think in broad strategic terms at this stage, and endeavour to clarify your initial thoughts about the possible location of the markets that offer you the best opportunity. These markets may not be distant exotic locations. Your best export market opportunity could be within a couple of hours flying time of your present location, or if you live on a major continent, it could be as close as just across the border!

First you should evaluate opportunities in a country close to your current country of operation, and then extend geographically outwards, on the premise that it is always less costly (and normally more time efficient) to commence your export programme in a 'near home' market.

This 'near home' decision almost always overcomes any major potential problems of cultural difference, and also often negates or reduces language difficulties. From a business control viewpoint, a 'near market' decision will certainly help you to accelerate market penetration as you will be able to afford to spend more time 'in-country' and less time (and cost) on travelling.

Why make things hard for yourself by travelling half way around the world to secure a new export market when an easier and more cost-effective opportunity may well be right on your own doorstep. Take a lead from the old IBM 'THINK' routine – 'THINK Cost - THINK Time – THINK Communications – THINK PROFIT!!!' A viable 'near market' decision makes good sense.

Sources of information

To assist you in your research process we list below many of the major sources of information which you should contact.

When contacting an organization, you should send a polite letter seeking information on potentials for exporters and enclose an A4 size pre-stamped and return addressed envelope. Over the past twenty years we cannot ever remember not receiving a reply to such a request.

The Internet has become extremely popular as a means for information distribution, but do not forget that it costs time and money for people to send information to you. It is usually far better to have the complete information in a well-presented hard copy format rather than a short précis of 'super-condensed' information. If you have a database on computer, and a scanner, you could scan the information into your database for further reference as required.

Information sources for new exporters

Local chamber of commerce	☐
Export section or group of a local chamber of commerce	☐
Business reference libraries	☐
Town or city hall business information departments	☐
Trade associations	☐
Regional government centres	☐
National government export departments	☐
National government department of trade	☐
Exporters associations	☐
Export agents	☐
International logistics providers	☐
Importers associations and agents	☐
Banks (they often have brochures and leaflets on exporting, particularly with regard to financial services and other financial information)	☐
Business schools and colleges	☐
Overseas governments	☐
Overseas governments' trade departments	☐
World Trade Centres	☐
Your country's overseas embassies	☐
Embassies, High Commissions and trade legations in your home country	☐

Tourist offices

Tourist information and tourist information packages which are available locally for your intended country of export are very useful. They often contain detailed city maps and additional information on hotels, culture, religion and many other topics of general and background interest. Furthermore, when you need to make overseas visits you may, if you are working with a very modest budget, wish to consider taking advantage of special holiday offers which cover your intended market. Many tour package hotels are situated right in the heart of major or capital cities. If you take a tour package you can reduce your business travel and accommodation costs by as much as 70 per cent.

The database

Unless you have a computer on which to record and index all your initial contacts, invest in a simple card file on which to record your new contacts. Treasure this list, and add to it, and continue to update it. You will be surprised in years to come how many times you will refer to this list. If you have an urgent problem, an 'in-country' contact is worth their weight in gold against starting right from cold. Even if your in-country contact cannot resolve your problem themselves, they almost certainly know someone who can help you, or at the very least they can point you in the right local direction.

If you record your contact information on a PC don't forget to file back-up routines on a regular basis. If you travel overseas do not under any circumstances take the 'master file' with you – only a copy. I learnt this lesson to my great cost many years ago, when my baggage and briefcase were stolen from a hotel room in the Far East. It took me over three years to re-compile the information contained in my export contact and reference list. In fact, I recovered less than 50 per cent of the list, and unfortunately lost contact with many good 'casual' overseas contacts for ever.

Never rely solely on memory. Furthermore, never trust electronic pocket notebooks for 'master' storage of contact information, regardless of the manufacturers' claims of 'total recoverability'. In reality, a motherboard failure means a total inability to recover the data.

Your first steps, therefore, should be to generate a quality information-seeking letter, schedule your business library and other commercial data visits, and commence your information gathering. As you progress, build up your own enquiry letter file database and index it into specific areas of interest or recipient category – one for embassies, one for chambers of commerce, one for exporters associations, business development agencies etc. This will save you an enormous amount of time in the future as you will be sending out many dozens of such letters over the forthcoming months.

EXECUTIVE BRIEFING
ON EXPORTING

INTRODUCTION

Having completed the steps outlined in Chapter 1 you should have amassed a considerable amount of information about overseas marketing, and begun to formulate some ideas on where your target markets could be located geographically. Index, record and file this information away for the present in your PC or filing cabinet; it will become of great use to you at a later stage when we commence creating your export business plan.

We now introduce you to the background briefing programme we use for the creation of exporting skills: the 'Executive Briefing on Exporting'. You may wish to include appropriate parts of this briefing in your internal management briefing on exporting which is described in more detail later in this chapter.

This executive briefing is not product or market sector specific. It explores a number of topics closely associated with exporting, and indicates some of the pitfalls to be avoided.

The prime reason for exporting is to achieve additional revenues and profit from the sale of your goods and services in overseas markets. We need to focus directly on this vital aspect of achieving sales before we address any other areas. You must ensure sales success with your export programme, if you are going to make any profit. This is the most vital part of the whole programme and should take precedence over everything else.

Before you start exporting you are understandably quite concerned about your chances of success, and about the potential costs involved. An export programme, whether large or small, will cost a considerable amount of money, and if you fail to achieve sales could have detrimental effects on your current home market business profitability. However, there are a number of ways in which to minimize this potential exposure.

RISK ASSESSMENT

The first part of the risk minimization assessment is for you to assess what potential financial exposure you could afford. At an absolute minimum (and using 1997 figures) it will cost $5000–$7000 to generate a small pilot scheme to test market or trial sale a non-complex single product or service in one 'near' overseas country. (Triple this amount if you want to explore a distant market.)

If you extend this small initial programme to a multi-product offering you will increase your base costs to a minimum of $10 000 (up to $20 000 if your intended market is half way round the world). If you wish to develop a modest agent or distribution network, this will on average cost between $10 000 and $30 000, depending on the range and scope of your activities and distance from your target market.

The cost of a more substantial and comprehensive export market entry programme commences at around $50 000, and can be as much as $500 000 for the first year of operation, particularly if you wish to set up a subsidiary company overseas, employ your own in-country sales and administrative staff and wish to undertake more comprehensive sales and marketing programmes. This sum does not include the cost of any form of professional advertising or media programme support; the cost of this could quite easily double this figure.

Deciding how much you would be prepared to write off if everything went completely wrong for you may not be a particularly positive approach, but it is realistic and does draw attention to the financial risks involved in exporting. It is better to make the assessment at the beginning than to proceed without it, only to face serious financial problems later.

You would be unwise to dismiss this advice, thinking that you could not suffer in this way, that you would manage your business better than this, or that those who have lost in the past failed through poor business skills. There are many examples of exporters who took great pains to do things correctly, and still lost considerable money through unforeseen circumstances. We have even known an appointed overseas agent sell off his principal's (unpaid-for) stock at knock-down prices in the local market to save himself from bankruptcy!

ASSESSING EXPORTING COSTS

Having now made some basic financial risk calculations and established your potential financial exposure, we now turn to another area where it is possible to minimize financial exposure, but which is often overlooked by potential exporters. This is knowing what your true exporting costs are.

All costs, either direct or indirect, associated with your export programme, must be totally separated from the accounting functions of your home country business, and must be capable of individual and separate audit. If you cannot measure your export programme in detailed financial terms you have no control of your export business and you have no way of knowing the potential impact of your export expenditure on the profits of your home country business.

Do not underestimate the necessity for this financial separation of export costs. Put this financial procedure into action immediately, before you commence any direct venture-funded exporting activity, and do not forget to include in your costs those of your research activity to date. They will have to be deducted from your export profits at some stage.

DEVELOPING A PROFESSIONAL EXPORT PROGRAMME

In the Introduction we stressed the absolute necessity for professional programme planning of overseas marketing activities. You will need all your skills in this area and you will also need to rely heavily on your people skills throughout the programme to ensure that your enthusiasm and commitment is extended to all of your management team, and to any of your staff involved with the programme. Returning to Herr Clausewitz for a moment: it is also important to secure your home base through staff commitment to your export programme, and as a professional manager you will recognize that it is people that make companies, not products. Enthusiastic management and staff commitment to your export programme is a vital ingredient for success.

How do you bring your financial planning activities, export programmes and business development projects together into one consolidated package? There are a number of options. You can proceed on your own, or you can seek varying degrees of professional assistance from a variety of exporting professionals, in developing your export business programme. We look first at the assistance available from various sources.

Export promotion events

One option is to take part in a chamber of commerce or government sponsored export promotion programme. Over the years we have seen a fair number of good results from such programmes – which have provided basic assistance to potential exporters at the start of their export business development programme.

However, export assistance programmes and events organized by these bodies have some drawbacks. These organizations cannot really assist you with direct and personalized business programmes to sell your products in overseas markets. The programmes developed by these organizations mainly concentrate on placing interested parties in touch with each other. It is usually down to the individual company and 'contact' to arrange everything else. A further possible drawback, in our experience on quite a number of occasions, is that although well intentioned, many of the organizers of such events have very little real 'hands-on' experience of professional export business generation programmes.

Thus, the value of such government or chamber of commerce export promotion programmes is limited to what they can provide in the briefing and initial assistance stage in the way of identifying potential markets, long distance introductions, and some local 'in country' information. Most of these organizations do not have the financial and budgetary resources available to comprehensively support individual company export business development promotions or export marketing programmes. Never lose sight of the primary need to establish sales of your own individual products in your targeted markets. This area of overseas business will always be directly related to your own efforts – with very little 'free' outside help available.

Professional exhibitions

Beware also of the 'professional' international exhibition and event organizers. In the main they have no interest whatsoever in your products or your company. Their interest is in staging a profitable exhibition, and their charges for stands or booths, pre-paid advertising (often of dubious quality) and for other stand 'services' such as telephone, stand erection, electricity and the provision of snacks and other hospitality items are invariably high.

A final point regarding such events concerns requests for a fully paid-up advance or a very substantial 'deposit' stand retainer fee many months before the event, on the grounds that 'we only reserve stands/booths after payment'. Unfortunately, there are unscrupulous operators in this field, as in others, and it is not unknown for would-be exhibitors to find that so-called event organizers have disappeared with all the deposit money. It is always wise to check with the exhibition venue, and find out for yourself whether they have a fully paid-up confirmed exhibition or event booking of your industry type for that date – in the same name as the published event organizers!

Selecting an export consultant

We strongly recommend that, right from the outset, you enlist the assistance of a professional, experienced export consultant who has confirmed and qualified experience of your targeted market.

Our own involvement in this field has shown us there are very few consultants with experience in the whole of the export process, from programme inception, to detailed 'in-country' experience, right through to professional market consolidation. There are plenty of first-class consultants of excellent reputation who specialize in various business sectors associated with exporting, but it is not easy to identify those with detailed and comprehensive practical 'in-country' experience of the total development of an export programme from absolute start-up situations.

We recommend that you seek advice and assistance from the contacts which you have developed in your initial export research. Many chambers of commerce have lists of qualified and experienced business consultants. This is usually a very good starting point. If you have a modem data-link, you can leave a 'note' in the postbox of the in-country chamber of commerce, and it is also worth accessing the international data networks such as Internet for names of suitable consultants who specialize in export business development in the business sector in which you are engaged.

Be very careful in your selection of an export consultant, as there are many so-called 'fringe' 'consultants' who will promise practical advice, special export support and 'personal' introductions, but who will not be able to fulfil these promises. You should always demand a reference list of at least three previous clients, whom you may contact. If your request is refused, perhaps on the grounds of client confidentiality, you should proceed no further with this 'consultant'.

Going it alone

It is perfectly possible to develop, generate and run an export programme by yourself. It will take time, application, money and effort, but with a committed and professional approach to your overseas marketing programme, you can certainly achieve an excellent result. It will take you considerably longer without professional assistance, and experience has indicated that there will probably not be significant savings in the overall cost.

CONFIRMATION OF COMMITMENT

We now review some of the questions which all potential exporters must face. These questions may be regarded by some as very blunt, as almost a direct intrusion on private and personal business ambitions. However, our practical experience has shown the value of such questions, relating to the involvement of an individual in the home market profit maximization programme, and to the personal, and sometimes more unsavoury aspects of exporting in terms of obtaining a 'confirmation of commitment' to the programme. Up to 30 per cent of people considering exporting opt out as a result of facing these questions. It is far better to opt out at this stage then to face bitter and possibly costly disappointment later in an export programme.

The questions that follow, which are based on 30 years' experience in international markets, review your personal ability to take on the rigours of a professional export programme.

The potential exporter's personal qualification question list

1 a Having read, and agreed, the principles of the home market profit optimization programme outlined in the Introduction, have you implemented any of the recommendations?

b If not, why not, especially if you have already agreed, and committed to this programme and recognized that this is the best way forward for you to increase base profit in your home market?

2 a Having implemented the home market profit optimization programme, have you been successful in generating more profit in your home market?

b If no, why do you think this is?

c If yes, have you generated additional profits in some areas and not in others, and if so, should you not go back and complete the rest of the profit optimization programme before you commence your export programme?

3a Is additional profit generation your real reason for exporting?

b If not, what other reasons do you have? Please list them.

c Do you truly believe that these are realistic reasons for commencing an export programme or are you really only guessing at a result? What evidence do you have that these reasons are realistic, practical and viable? Or is it the thought of fully expensed and tax-free foreign travel to exotic lands which attracts, and excites you, rather than the practical exporting programme objectives?

4a How much involvement does your personal ego have in this decision? Be honest!

b Do you truly believe that you have the capability, or the dedicated intent of purpose to become a professional international businessman or woman, or is this really only part of a personal image 'wish' list?

5a Do you have an ulterior personal motive for exporting, perhaps a desire to get away from current business or family relationship pressures, or to indulge yourself in an expensive 'jet-set' lifestyle?

b Do you believe that there is any element of 'escapism' in your approach to exporting?

6   Have you the personal, or committed and approved, company financial resources to embark upon a potentially expensive export business programme, and be able to 'write it off' without serious personal or commercial consequences if things go wrong?

7   Exporting can be, and almost always is, very physically and mentally demanding. Do you believe that you have the capacity for very long hours of work coupled with extensive travel, to take a great deal of 'multi-tasking' pressure, and that you have the personal physical and mental strength to survive long term in this very demanding environment?

8 a   If you had to directly pay someone else to carry out this programme for you, what would you demand of them in terms of personal commitment, attributes and contribution? Please list these requirements.

b   Will you have the strength of personality to demand this from yourself?

9 a   You will almost certainly have to spend considerable time away from your wife/husband, partner, children, family and friends. Do you consider that you have a sufficiently strong personal relationship with these people, that you will be able to overcome the separation factors, and to sustain these relationships without severe impact on your long-term personal relationship with them?

b   Have you talked to them about the possibility of being apart for considerable periods of time?

c   What was their reaction?

10   If you are going to export to less developed countries, you are almost certainly going to become ill at some stage, and quite possibly hospitalized. Disease and infections are often a great deal more vicious in some parts of the world than at home, especially in the tropics, and particularly in many third world countries. Will you be able to cope with this possible eventuality, far from home and quite often entirely on your own?

11   You will almost certainly have to spend many long hours in aircraft, often in conditions very different from the stability, luxury and safety of an intercontinental 747. There will almost certainly be some very rough rides in small aircraft in remote places. Are you able to face this with a degree of confidence?

12   If you plan to visit third world countries and particularly some of the more underdeveloped countries, you will be exposed to many disturbing and upsetting sights. Poverty, malnutrition, disease, and even public display of dead and dying human beings are common in many of these countries. Do you think that you will be able to come to terms with this?

13a   At some stage of an extensive exporting career your personal safety and security, even possibly your life, may be endangered through a criminal act upon your person, or through attempted theft of your belongings. Do you really believe that you can look after yourself? Remember, the world does not stop outside the entrance to a five star hotel!

   b   How 'streetwise' are you?

14   What evidence can you provide of your personal self-sufficiency, and your ability to make the best of things in difficult, and often hostile environments? Please list.

Please complete all of the above questions as honestly as you can, and then file away your answers for a couple of days, to enable you to 'stand back' from the questions and the situations posed therein, and to enable you to analyze your responses with a degree of objectivity.

If, after due consideration, you feel that the potential personal demands of exporting are more than you feel comfortable with, it is better to draw a line at this point, and for you to concentrate on the maximum development of your home market. You might decide to discontinue your direct personal involvement in the export programme at this point, or perhaps delay your full commitment decision to a later date. If you decide that some of the potential personal problems are insurmountable, you are strongly recommended to seek alternative export programme arrangements. This is quite justifiable, completely understandable and a very mature and sensible approach.

We know of many people with broken marriages, ulcers and stress disorders, and people who have lost a great deal more money than they really could afford – people who have taken on exporting lightly, and lived to regret it.

However, there is a further option for you to consider. It is possible to continue with initiating an export programme, but with a reduced involvement from yourself, if you are able to identify a suitable member of staff within your organization to take on this role. You may be able to delegate front-line responsibility at the beginning, enabling you to delay your own involvement until the intended market is more stable and established.

If, however, you believe that you are able to take on a major overseas business commitment, the rest of this book is your personal guide and way forward to successfully cracking overseas markets.

Having taken, and totally committed yourself to, this final and most important personal decision, you are now ready to proceed with the overseas market entry programmes contained in this book. These programmes will assist you in every way possible to succeed in your new markets.

We now commence the structured programme for export market entry.

INTRODUCING MANAGEMENT AND STAFF
TO EXPORTING

There are three ways of introducing major changes, represented by the following statements.

'Order me – and I will just do what is required.'

'Request me – and I will assist, without knowledge.'

'Explain to me and involve me – and I will move heaven and earth to help you!'

Let the last of the above maxims guide you when presenting your new overseas business programmes to your management and staff. Having a good team, fully committed by involvement, education and training, is the best possible way to commence your programme. The following chapters show you how to plan to ensure the all-round involvement and commitment of your staff.

A vital part of this structured programme is the management and staff export briefing. You generally only get one chance to carry this out, so you have to do it correctly. Considerable preparation is required, as most people do not like surprises, especially when they have potential impact on their jobs, and the structure of their workplace. How would you like suddenly to be told that substantial changes are about to take place, that you will probably have to learn new skills, and to meet significant challenges? That would certainly worry me, as I am sure it would you.

The best way to introduce change, under normal controlled circumstances, is to do so progressively. It is even better if the ideas for change come from your own management and staff. From the viewpoint of a member of staff usually the best ideas are those they have generated themselves! As a start, a new business development ideas programme implemented through your line managers is as good a place to start as any.

Commence your new overseas business programme by briefing your managers on the need to progressively develop the business over the next few years to ensure future prosperity for all involved in the company – from senior directors to new starters. Stress how important it is to secure additional market share, and to be stronger and more professional than the competition. State how vital it is that every single member of staff should have the opportunity to make a contribution to these aims, and to be able to put forward their own ideas. Brief your management team well on this topic and ensure the following message gets across: 'The company is actively seeking additional ways in which to grow and prosper, and wishes to involve all of its staff in formulating new business generation programmes.'

This initial management and supervisor ('M & S') briefing should be followed soon after by staff briefings on the same topic. The ideas and recommendations generated by staff present at these meetings should be noted and recorded. The ideas which come from such discussions can sometimes be extremely valuable. It is almost certain that a number of staff will have asked about the possibilities which are present in export markets. If they did not, it is more than likely that you did not include the right prompts in the 'M & S' briefing.

Having received a number of concrete suggestions, you should approach those people who made suggestions and invite them to join an export evaluation task force. The wider the spread across departments, the better it will be for you later on as the programme develops towards implementation. Appoint an experienced manager to head the task force to co-ordinate all activities and to compile initial suggestions regarding an export plan. If your company is very small take the lead role yourself – but still try not to overlook the input of any member of your staff.

The above briefing programme should ensure an excellent start, and first class commitment by your staff to an export programme. Follow up the initial export programme 'launch' activities with a formal management statement of intent confirming the company's desire to seriously evaluate the company's export potentials, and let everyone know about the staff task force. Request the manager heading the task force to issue a weekly note of progress that will be placed on all staff notice boards, discussed at staff meetings, and for general distribution. Remember that all departments must be informed.

One company we know well, which wished to commence an export programme to mainland Europe from the UK, did not bother to involve any of the staff in its transport section with the export briefing. Little did they know – until very much later in the programme – that they had a part-time, semi-retired van driver employed on local deliveries who had spent the last thirty years of his mainstream career driving long-distance trucks all around Europe, and who, as a result, had a wealth of knowledge of all the problems associated with Euro-freighting.

Never forget that everyone, and anyone – regardless of their position, status or seniority in the company – potentially has a part to play in a professional export business development programme.

If you have not compiled a list of the 'additional skills and previous experience' of all your employees, it is time that you did so. We are confident that you will be amazed at the wide variety of 'untapped' skills (such as foreign languages) which are potentially available to you.

EXPORT COSTS

We return briefly to a topic raised earlier in this chapter: export costs. It is essential to remember that you must know the costs of your exports. Exporting takes time, resources and money. You will not be able to make a single penny of profit from your new export until your goods or services have been sold and paid for.

Remember always to keep separate the cost and accounting procedures of your export programme, and review your export programme expenditure at least once a month. This way you will be fully aware, and in control of any export cost escalations, and will be able immediately to identify, and to analyze the potential impact which this expenditure may have on your home-generated profits through 'consolidated' accounting practices. Knowing your true export costs is half the battle.

■ Example

A successful UK exporter, an owner director, had developed his own export programme, worked hard at it, and sold quite a volume of his product in the US market. During a discussion about export programmes, we outlined a short form analysis programme for comparing export profits to export costs, which we use to evaluate true profits in new overseas markets.

He soon realized that, because his product was a relatively low cost one, with only medium margin, it would be many years before he actually made a 'positive' profit against his total 'real and actual' accumulated export costs to date.

THE COMPANY FITNESS PROGRAMME: EVALUATING A COMPANY'S EXPORT SKILLS

INTRODUCTION

We now turn our attention to how best to modify or enhance your present company structure in preparation for exporting. Almost every company which has enlisted our services to assist with exporting problems has omitted this vital preparatory stage.

Such preparation dramatically reduces the likelihood that the export programme will be hindered by internal problems. Every company which is new to exporting must go through an internal export evaluation and skills assessment programme. This programme will cover almost every department in the company, and will assess current capabilities, and identify those areas of current business practice or methods which need to be amended or restructured to meet the demands of exporting.

This process – although quite detailed – does not take a great deal of time and effort, provided you have the checklists to work with. This chapter contains the checklists that will enable you to conduct your own 'readiness to export' analysis and review.

There are a number of main areas in almost every company that need to be addressed, evaluated and potentially 'upgraded' to bring them to readiness for exporting. The first task is to list all the departments in your company and compare it with the checklist below.

Main areas to evaluate for readiness to export

1 **The sales department**   ☐

2 **The marketing department**   ☐

3 **The finance and legal department**   ☐

4 **Data processing and information systems department**   ☐

5 **The logistics department**   ☐

6 **Quality control/standards department**   ☐

You will also need to make arrangements with some other external business providers which are necessary for exporting, such as your company bank, your company solicitor and your company travel agent and so on.

Further additional areas which will possibly need to be covered in the assessment programme are set out in the following checklist.

Secondary departments for assessment

1 **Production department** ☐

2 **Product development** ☐

3 **Dispatch department** ☐

4 **Procurement/purchasing department** ☐

5 **Training department** ☐

6 **Personnel department** ☐

7 **Word processing/secretarial** ☐

8 **Directors and/or vice-presidents** ☐

We now need to address some of these areas individually to provide you with the key points which need to be addressed on an individual departmental basis. You will no doubt have already recognized that the sales department is top of the list. Remember our opening remarks: 'This book makes no apologies for focusing closely on export sales.'

SALES DEPARTMENT

The depth to which you go to prepare your sales department for exporting depends on the sales distribution route you take in your preferred export market. There are a number of alternatives, all of which require varying degrees of direct sales involvement or sales support.

You will not yet have had the opportunity to fully evaluate the best route for you, from your sales distribution alternatives of direct sales, agent sales, distributor sales, joint venture or partnership sales arrangements. However, the above sales distribution alternatives form two groups, each of which requires a slightly different approach for exporting. As this book has been written to be non-specific as regards product type, geographical location and market sector, we have combined these evaluation processes into one, which should enable you to cover almost all requirements.

Regardless of which sales distribution route you finally decide upon, the structure, professionalism and commitment of your sales staff is going to play a vital role in your overall export result. As you will no doubt appreciate from the personal evaluation and the confidential review of personal skills discussed in Chapter 2, not everyone, for a whole variety of reasons, is suitable for a role within export sales.

It is appropriate here to point out that there are some countries in which attitudes to women involved in business differ from those in the developed western world.

Sales structure

If your company at present has only a single 'home' based sales organization, this must be changed. Not only will you need to separate out all of the sales costs associated with exporting (and you cannot do this easily if sales staff are combining home and export market activities), but you will also need to create a sales environment where total focus on export sales is achievable.

We recommend that, if it is financially possible, you create a totally separate sales function for export sales staff. In our opinion the skills and personal qualities required by a successful export sales person are of a magnitude considerably higher than those of sales staff in home market environments. In our view, any appointments from current sales staff to the role of export sales, should be considered as promotions. Remember – export sales markets are almost always considerably tougher than home markets; you need the most competent, most experienced people in there fighting for sales for you. We will cover export sales motivation, long-distance management control and direction in Chapter 19. At the beginning it is best to concentrate on getting the key sales players in place.

Sales forecasts and prospect lists

Every company needs a first class sales prospect evaluation and sales forecast system. Collect all the information on your current sales forecast and prospect system and review it in depth. You will almost certainly need to develop a new sales prospect list and forecast system for export sales. The full details of how to create, and implement, a professional export sales prospect and evaluation system are provided in Chapter 18.

All too often a sales prospect list is subject to what is referred to as the 'rule of three'. Briefly, this rule relates to the progressive scaling down of prospect quotas or targets at each stage of the management hierarchy, so as to ensure that targets are entirely realistic and achievable. It is rare for any company to consistently, week by week, month by month, and quarter by quarter, fully achieve its projected and documented forward sales forecast.

The impact of the sales forecast on home market sales projections and forecasts is repeated in relation to export markets thousands of miles away. Just one of the complicating factors of the export market is that quite often pre-shipment has to take place against a forecast for the goods, products or services to arrive by the customer's required delivery time.

MARKETING DEPARTMENT

Your marketing staff will most likely have concentrated almost totally on home markets to date. However, they must now become involved in a number of activities to support the sales thrust into new export markets. Any work they may previously have done, in assessing export market potential, is likely to be out of date and irrelevant. The international markets in many product sectors have changed considerably over the past few years, with new markets emerging, and traditional markets becoming re-structured. You have only to take a close look at the impact of the European Community market, and the emergence of the Pacific Rim market on global market distribution to see what we mean.

Involving the marketing department requires, at the outset, a clarification of the lines of responsibility of sales and marketing departments in the export business development programme.

It is the responsibility of sales personnel to sell the product. This involves the total sales process, from initial customer contact and follow-up, right through to completing the final paperwork – after the sale is completed. It also includes the progressive development of a first-class prospect system, and all sales management, control, direction and motivation of staff, whether direct sales or sales support staff.

Almost everything else should fall within the control of the marketing department. The fact that they are not paid commission on sales means that they are more unbiased than sales staff and are thus usually more objective in their assessments of sales issues – particular with regard to any variations on special deal margin calculations.

Activities which should be directly controlled by the marketing department within the export business programme are: all market research, management of product development programmes or product enhancement activities, marketing programmes, advertising and media programmes, sales promotion, sales brochures and technical information sheets, and the most difficult issue – pricing and discount structures.

We strongly recommend that all new products be pre-verified as viable products by sales personnel, as there are many examples of excellent products which, for one reason or another, the sales force found to be limited or non saleable in the market-place.

Ideally, a professional 'sales based' market appraisal programme, and price performance evaluation instigated by the marketing department throughout the product development cycle, should be carried out. Unfortunately, very few companies have the foresight to implement such a programme. The alternative is to evaluate the product after it is produced, but before launch.

The best technique we have found for doing this is to put three or four of your most experienced sales people into a hotel for a day, with not ungenerous expenses. Rent a conference room, and include secretarial support. Give them the objective of a 'no holds barred' independent sales evaluation of the product, let them elect their own team leader, and let them get on with it. We think that you could be very surprised at the outcome.

FINANCE DEPARTMENT

You can be very successful in selling your goods and services in overseas markets, make excellent headway with sales and marketing programmes, and begin to carve yourself a market share, but all of these achievements are totally useless unless you get paid.

There can be a difference of opinion whether sales or finance staff are responsible for getting the invoices paid. In exporting we believe that it should be the primary responsibility of the finance department to ensure, not only that you are paid in full for your goods and services, but also that you are paid promptly. The finance department should therefore be involved at a very early stage in all contractual negotiations which involve payments, or terms and conditions associated with payments. We also recommend that the finance department act as watchdog in all aspects of margin calculations produced by the marketing department for use in sales proposals, quotations etc. It is usually only within the finance department that accurate reconciliation can take place of true costs against sale price – for true margin determination.

■ Example

During the last twenty years we have been associated with many companies for export programme implementation and business development in both European and global markets. One company, which had devised and implemented its own market entry programme, requested additional support to expand into a new market some 5000 miles from their corporate home base. We completed a company profiling module, and a lead product group evaluation. This contained product margin analysis data. As we always do, we ran this data against the software programs we have developed, which automatically input numeric values to compensate for differing geographic factors. We usually obtain fairly consistent 'average' results, but this evaluation indicated a projected accumulated loss. We ran it several times, each time slightly increasing the 'what if' factors, but there remained a substantial down trend.

Further examination, with close support and input from the client's finance section, indicated the following:

1 The company marketing department had calculated its export margins on home sales margins plus an estimated ten per cent for export overheads.

2 They had not taken into account term stockholding by distributors; we subsequently found that the distributors had negotiated over-generous demonstration stock facilities from sales and were selling 'demonstration stock' short and holding the cash long!

3 Although the cost of sales for export (travel overheads, etc.) had been reasonably accurately costed, no sales support costs (i.e. technical product support) had been included.

4 No calculations had been included for insurance during transit (although the products were small high value goods that are easily stolen).

5 Anticipated customer payments had been 'pre-converted' into US dollars on a fixed pre-agreed rate which was found to be substantially to the company's disadvantage.

6 The finance department had had only a very brief involvement in the preparation of the sales proposals and margin calculations (essentially, only the provision of raw data and base costs). The sales proposal calculations were found to be inadequate to support the expected margins.

7 Local in-country advertising and sales promotion was coming direct from the corporate marketing budget, as were the direct mail programme and the literature and technical information documentation.

8 'In-country' training costs for distributors and 'customer key-trainers' had not been included anywhere.

Almost everyone at the company was under the impression that the programme was proceeding to plan.

This was a fine example of too many people being involved in exporting, with non-related or correlated budgets. Above all, there was a basic lack of budgetary co-ordination and fiscal control from the outset. This should have been provided by means of a direct control programme from the finance department.

You must know where *all* your true costs are when exporting.

DATA PROCESSING AND INFORMATION SYSTEMS DEPARTMENT

Today almost every company, from the smallest 'sole owner' venture to the largest of the multinationals uses computer support in one way or another. The following comments should, therefore, be considered mandatory reading, as the major principles reviewed are common to almost all computer users.

Whether you have a large or a small computer system, even if you have only one or two PCs for accounting and stock control, there is one major problem to be overcome within your computing facility. This is the ability to separate your export finance from your home-market day to day transactions. The larger the system, the more complex this will be. This may not be a significant problem for an operation with a simple stand-alone PC, but in larger operations it will be almost impossible to totally separate export financial information, because of interaction with current home-market programmes such as stock control etc., which requires a common database type approach to ensure information integrity. In such cases you may need to create new 'export only' databases to support your overseas programme.

LOGISTICS DEPARTMENT

Logistics (taking in the functions of goods inwards/outwards, dispatch, warehousing and transport) play a vital role in the operations of many companies, and have a very bright technology-based future. Logistics are essential to an export programme, and in many companies, a complete new logistics industry has developed from a relatively low-tech past to become a major force supporting both their national and their global distribution. Not all companies yet have a separate logistics department or section, however, and for smaller companies it may be more cost-effective to use the services of an established international logistics expert (such as DHL, TNT or Federal Express), which offers a complete 'logistics package', than to employ your own specialist staff, find forwarding agents, arrange transport etc.

The following checklist sets out the functions that a logistics operation must provide.

Logistics department checklist

1 Special packing, boxing, pallets, and/or hard crating. ☐

2 Methods of storage. ☐

3 Export documentation and certificates, including compliance with health and safety requirements. ☐

4 Transportation to customs/point of dispatch from home country. ☐

5 Onward transportation, including in-country transportation to point of delivery. ☐

6 Any special requirements for hazardous goods. ☐

7 Appointment of forwarders and shippers. ☐

8 Logistics – export management and control systems. ☐

QUALITY CONTROL/STANDARDS DEPARTMENT

A quality control and standards department has an important role to play in an export programme, to ensure, not only that the quality of goods or services meets all necessary in-country commercial and customer requirements, but most importantly, that electrical, safety and other in-country industry standards are fully complied with.

Without a full appreciation of standards and certification requirements, and the points necessary for compliance in the desired country of distribution, it will be impossible to sell your goods and services, as in many cases either it will be illegal to do so, or it will break in-country established codes of practice.

One area where there are particular problems in relation to standards and documentation is within the 'high tech' industry sector. In addition to various government restrictions relating to exportation of high technology, most products within the high technology sector these days require connectivity to networks or other original equipment manufacturer (OEM) systems. This is especially so within the data or voice transmission industry: telephone products and network devices are very good examples of this. 'In-country' product certification is almost always required for these products and obtaining this may take considerable time. If you are also forced to use in-country certification houses, the costs associated with this process can be astronomic. One company had to delay its product launch by one and a half years to achieve in-country certification – and were quoted one million dollars for the complete certification process which would have cost not more than $200 000 in their own country.

You should not depend on bilateral or cross-border product certification agreements between various countries. Our experience has shown that such arrangements are subject to a great deal of interpretation (usually by the country which is financially advantaged by a high-cost certification process) and all may not be what it seems initially.

With regard to external business providers which are necessary to your export programme, the following comments may be useful.

THE BANK

Your company bankers should be well placed to assist you with your export programme. Go and talk to them and seek their advice. Many of the larger banks have complete 'national' departments concerned solely with export support. If you are with a small banking organization it is recommended that you consider moving your banking to one of the large banking organizations which will be much better placed to assist, guide and support you.

YOUR COMPANY LAWYER

Many small companies have long standing arrangements with a local lawyer but small local law firms often do not have the volume of work to support an international department. However, international law is so complex that it is essential that you have access to proper advice, experience and facilities. You must ensure that your lawyer is able to provide these.

Resorting to international law is a very expensive procedure and not to be recommended unless a great deal of money is at stake. It is far better to write into your international sales contracts a clause regarding arbitration procedures, rather than to rush to an international lawyer if a dispute becomes inevitable.

If you do not already have a good international company lawyer appointed or on a modest retainer, now is the time to appoint one.

TRAINING
REQUIREMENTS

You cannot expect a quality export performance from your staff without adequate training. They need to understand in detail not only what they are doing, and how to do it, but also the reason why it is necessary. This not only applies to exporting, but also to almost all work situations – regardless of market sector, product or service type, level of job complexity, or position in the management hierarchy of a company. Almost all staff respond to, and respect, additional training to assist them to do a good job. The export training programme set out below will help to fulfil these identified needs.

IDENTIFYING TRAINING REQUIREMENTS AND PRIORITIES

The key training elements for exporting, which need to be addressed across the whole company are as follows.

1 **A good general briefing on the new export programme for all staff.**

2 **An explanation of why exporting is important to the company's long-term prosperity and financial success.**

3 **A definition and identification of the role and contribution of the individual within the export programme.**

4 **The need for good teamwork.**

5 **The assessment of export training requirements.**

6 **A comprehensive training programme for each department or key individual.**

7 **A defined time scale and calendar of events for training.**

8 **Management control, focus, and direction of the training programme.**

Obviously, there is a great deal to be accomplished in a training programme, so early identification of key export training requirements is fundamental to success.

In general, it is best to link your staff export training requirements directly to the strategic export business plan implementation programme. This gives you a time scale within which to complete the necessary training programmes in order to initiate the physical exporting of your products or services.

There are some readily defined areas, individuals and departments of the company which will require longer time scales than others for export training. It is important to identify and address these areas early in the export training programme to enable you to bring everything together in the correct order to provide comprehensive administrative and operational support for your export programme.

Training requirements and priorities differ from company to company, depending on factors such as individual market sector, product type etc. There are a number of functions which are common to almost all companies, and which should always be included in the first part of the export training programme. These are as follows.

QUALITY AND STANDARDS

It is extremely important that all requirements for quality and standards conformance for the targeted export market are recognized at an early stage and addressed. These standards requirements will almost certainly have an impact on production, so it is vital to establish any additional specialist training requirements for quality or standards right at the beginning of the export training programme.

Additional training may also be required to interpret standards conformance and the standards documentation of a foreign country. In addition to this, it may be necessary to learn and to implement enhanced measurement and quality analysis skills.

The area of quality and standards is fundamental to exporting success, as failure to meet technical or safety standards will severely delay, or could possibly even cancel, the whole export programme for your company.

Those who are engaged in service industries need to apply a similar process in relation to contracts and in-country legal requirements or accepted methods of working.

It is also pertinent at this point to offer a reminder regarding some aspects of product certification. Although any additional training requirements are minimal – as the certification process is always completed by outside professionals (regardless of the country in which it takes place) – it is a very good idea to review this matter within the context of training for the standards and quality control department, as some additional skills may have to be learnt, particularly if a product certification process has never been undertaken previously.

Certification can take between six and 18 months depending on product complexity, the number of product variations to be certified (with each variation usually requiring individual certification), and the availability of home or 'in-country' certification engineers. In addition to this, if you are proposing to export products to a number of different countries, be aware that each country may require its own product certification process to be completed. This can become a very expensive exercise.

EXPORT DOCUMENTATION AND FINANCIAL INSTRUMENTS

The area of export documentation and finance is extraordinarily complex. Documentation is required for the physical movement of goods, and the range of financial instruments, methods of payment etc. is bewildering. Throughout the world, there are literally thousands of regulations, rules, restrictions and conditions which apply to exporters and importers of products or services. What may be totally suitable, legal, morally acceptable or correct in one country may be totally unacceptable in another. This even applies within the Common Market in Europe as the Directives of the European Commission are left to individual countries to interpret and apply.

The problems in relation to the physical movement of goods (and services) between countries are compounded in the case of restricted, dangerous or hazardous goods, or those which may be regarded as morally suspect in some countries.

If your goods fall into any of these categories, your costs may be much higher than you had initially estimated, so you should be prepared. In addition, you may need to make provision for special training – especially if your goods are on the International Air Freight Hazardous Goods list.

In addition to the problems relating to the physical movement of goods and services, potential exporters also face a great variety of methods of payment, special export insurance and payment options.

As you will no doubt appreciate from the above, training in export documentation and financial arrangements is lengthy and difficult. It is not much use closing an export contract if your goods never get shipped, or are held indefinitely in Customs (either in your own country or in the country of destination), or even worse, if due to a major error in financial arrangements or payment documentation, you never get paid!

As stated in the Introduction, the documentation and regulation of the export process is complex and fraught with difficulties. It is not the province for well-meaning amateurs. Professional advice on export documentation and finance is available but no one individual can have a comprehensive and detailed knowledge of every market. We most strongly recommend independent professional training in export documentation and finance.

Most banks, financial institutions, accountants, export councils and chambers of commerce will normally be only too happy to advise you on the local availability of training in export documentation and export finance, and will usually endeavour to assist you to define and qualify the export documentation requirements for your targeted market. Do not forget also to speak to your own financial director or chief accountant, as they – through membership of their own professional body – may be able to seek help and advice upon this subject.

You should also write direct to your own country's embassy or trade legation in your targeted country of export and seek their advice on import/export regulations. You should contact them in any case, but their value in this context is that they often have additional unpublished local information and directives on import/export regulations. Your immediate compliance with these local regulations/directives often goes a long way to help smooth the export/import process when your products or goods finally arrive at their point of importation into a foreign country. Your initial approach to your home country embassy for information also sets up a direct line of communication with the embassy's commercial and trade department, which will prove invaluable in the future, particularly if difficulties are experienced.

As it takes a long time to learn about export documentation and export finance you should ensure that this area of training is scheduled early in your programme. If your company is of modest size and means, and does not have the administrative infrastructure to support all aspects of direct export, you are recommended to seek the assistance and advice of one of the major international logistics companies. As mentioned in Chapter 3, most of these companies now offer 'complete solution' packages for exporters. Although such packages may appear to be somewhat expensive, you are virtually assured of getting your products to the required destination in a saleable condition. If your products are relatively small and fairly lightweight, and have a high unit value, an international logistics company's services offer a very viable alternative to 'going it alone' (particularly if your goods have high unit value) as their global 'Goods in Transit' security arrangements are usually excellent. It is, in any case, a good idea to talk with them – as you are sure to need some support from them at some time with urgent deliveries or very small shipment quantities which do not qualify for bulk shipment rates.

Another service offered by many of these companies is specialist training courses for your staff, using their own methodology of international shipment and logistics support. Some even provide you free of charge with a specially programmed PC which gives direct terminal access to their international logistics and distribution system. Additional training will be required if you intend to pursue this route of product distribution and logistics support.

SALES ADMINISTRATION

More problems are generated in sales administration than any other area of exporting. Mistakes within this area can have more far-reaching effects than those in almost any other area of export procedures.

One of the main problems appears to be the lack of understanding of export contract terminology (e.g., contract clauses and conditions), and the failure to appreciate the possible implications of decisions taken (quite often in isolation from the export process). This is a most important area, especially if you are bidding for an export contract against a tender published overseas. For those of you who wish to examine this topic in more detail, make a start with two of the potentially problematic areas – *offsets*, and *buy-back*. If you do not know what these terms mean, go to the local library or chamber of commerce and look them up.

Again, as in the area of export documentation and export finance, we believe that training in export contract negotiation should be undertaken by training professionals. Courses are available on export contract negotiation and contract interpretation. A good place to start for advice is right in your own company, with your purchasing manager or procurement director. They deal with all types of supply and procurement contracts on an almost daily basis, and, if they are members of a professional institute of purchasing, procurement or supply, they will almost certainly have direct access through their institute membership to some high quality training in dealing with commercial export contracts, and in export contract negotiation techniques.

We should like to digress for a moment, and bring to your attention another important point within export sales administration. Never send an untrained and unseasoned export sales person overseas on their own to conduct final contract negotiations to point of signature, without the back-up of an export contract professional. If you do not have such back-up, you may end up paying your overseas customers for the privilege of sending them your products!

SALES TRAINING

Sales staff face significant problems in selling to export markets. It is easy to understand and readily sympathize with a sales person's focused and dedicated approach to getting the business signed. Almost all sales people consider that the only real evidence of their success is a signed contract. If they do not come home with an export contract they know that they will probably experience openly (or implied) cynical remarks about having a nice overseas holiday on the company's time and money! However, it is far better to have no contract than a bad contract, and anyone who tries to denigrate sales staff for failing to obtain a contract should be reminded of this in no uncertain terms.

Selling overseas is totally different from selling in your home country. The people your sales staff meet overseas often differ very greatly from those they meet in home markets. The overseas customers may have different attitudes to business, a different culture and, sometimes, different standards of business ethics.

While we are on this subject, we have to admit that everyone in the export business is generally out to get the best deal they possibly can. There are many examples of sales staff making costly errors on behalf of their companies through their over-keenness to get a contract signed before their return home.

An experienced overseas importer/buyer will know that a salesperson's time is limited in his or her country, and will often delay negotiations (usually by cultural appreciation trips, late-night entertaining, and other distractions) as late as possible in order to put pressure on the seller to come to some arrangement before departure. A short time for negotiation means inadequate attention to contract closing in most cases.

The availability of good quality training for export sales staff is extremely limited. It seems that this is one area where long and extensive overseas sales experience is the only real answer, as trading conditions, environments, commercial, cultural and other factors vary so much from country to country, and from continent to continent.

If you are committing your company to an extensive regionally focused export programme, we strongly recommend that you either send one of your current (high-energy, high-performance) sales staff to the targeted country of export for extended in-country experience before the beginning of the export programme, or recruit a new member for your sales team with current, comprehensive experience of living and selling in your targeted country. (Ideally this should be a national of the target country.)

Regardless of which of these options you finally settle for, make a small but important investment in your export sales programme by purchasing good quality language tuition for your export sales staff (either a self-learning course using internationally renowned materials, such as those of the International Linguaphone Institute or a course run by a recognised language school) so that they develop at least a rudimentary knowledge of the local language.

A small word of advice in relation to conducting sales negotiations with bilingual in-country buyers, especially within group environments: whatever your knowledge of the language, it is quite often to your advantage to profess virtually little or no understanding of the local language. This may enable you to pick up information let slip by the other side in their own language at business meetings and when socializing, when they believe you are totally unable to understand them. Please, however, respect this advice in the 'safety precaution' manner it is intended, and do not under any circumstances abuse your hosts' hospitality.

SELECTING STAFF TRAINING FOR EXPORTING

The discussion earlier in this chapter, and in Chapter 3, has indicated that there are some areas of training which we consider should always be addressed by professional trainers who are specialists in their areas of export knowledge, regulations and procedures.

Export documentation and export finance are examples of these specialist knowledge areas. Due to the complexity and sheer size of these issues, we have not dealt with them in any detail. Furthermore, the constantly changing nature of export documentation and regulations, means that whatever we could have written upon this topic would have been out of date within twelve months. It is vital that you use only current and valid information, so, even if you have the 'latest' information, make sure that you have the latest official updates as well.

We believe strongly that 'a little knowledge is dangerous' in these more complex administrative areas of exporting, and that, in almost all circumstances, time has proven the wisdom of our recommendation to engage professional support.

If you dislike the idea of seeking specialist support, and are of the opinion you are personally quite capable of doing without any professional training, please take a little time to complete the following exercise.

Visit your local business library and chamber of commerce reference section, and look up the current publication list of available information on export finance and export documentation. After doing this, please write to your government export trade department and ask them to send you their list of current information and published documentation on this topic.

You will now almost certainly have a list approaching, or even in excess of, one hundred information documents or publications that will take you years to read through, assimilate and understand. We believe that it is far better for you to put your pride in your pocket on this topic, and bow to the years of professional experience that go into the compilation of such documents, and go straight for professional training as the first, preferred and only really viable option.

Having now done some promotion for professional trainers, and evaluated some of the more complex areas of training requirements, let us now look at some of the other areas of training which are required for success in exporting, and review how we may best approach them. As in most areas, you either pay or 'do it yourself'.

We now look at a number of training options open to you. In addition to describing the various options available, we integrate these options into a single recommendation in order to cover all sizes of companies and their greatly varying internal training capabilities. In real terms there is not a great deal of difference in the content between the various options reviewed, but there is a considerable difference in the cost between specialist (bought-in expertise) and 'home grown' programmes.

The three major areas of training requirements which need to be addressed are:

1 Specialist knowledge areas (i.e. export documentation and export finance).

2 Special requirements for individual departments (i.e. standards and quality).

3 Training of individual staff in additional exporting skills which are directly related or complementary to their current role.

The three main training options available to you are:

1 Buy in a 'total solution' training package from a quality professional training company which will cover all identified requirements and aspects of your export training programme.

2 Buy in professional training to meet the more complex exporting training requirements, and then create a secondary programme yourself to cover the remaining areas.

3 Define your requirements and produce your own in-house export training programme.

The recommended option in almost all cases is option 2. This is a combination of contracted-out professional training skills married with your own internal or personal training skills, in order to produce the most cost-effective option.

APPOINTMENT OF KEY TRAINERS

Any training by outside professional trainers tends to be rather an expensive business. Thus, it is in your best interest to maximize your investment in training, by ensuring that the knowledge gained by a participating member of your staff is available for cross-training transfer to other members of staff in your organization, as additional back-up.

When you sign a contract for professional training, it is important to negotiate an additional clause into the training contract that allows you to use some of the course material internally to assist with the training of 'back-up' staff. This does not mean wholesale duplication of all the course manuals and training materials (the copyright of which is usually held by the training company anyway), but the use of some of the course material for training 'second-level' staff, and to provide 'back-up' support in case of sickness or holidays, or to cover the departure of a fully trained member of staff at very short notice. In this connection, it is worth ensuring that, if your operation is 'tight' on staffing, all key staff within your organization are under term contracts, or are required to give realistic notice of departure. We recommend three months as the minimum notice period for most staff, and six months for key players in the export process.

If possible, always endeavour to select a member of your staff for specialist training who has an identifiable capability for teaching and instructing, to enable them to pass on their knowledge. If you go about this in the right way from the beginning, you will build a 'treasure house' of key trainers, which will stand you in good stead in the future as your export business expands.

If the size of your company allows for a separate personnel department, always involve them in this process, and let them develop a professional programme for internal and external training. In the future this may then be easily expanded into a formal sub-section of the personnel department – the training department.

If you complete this initial staff training programme as described above, you will not have to recruit any additional trainers to staff this new department, as you will have developed your own process of internal vertical integration for training, further developed current staff with additional exporting skills, and already have a 'pool' of training resources to draw upon as instructors for this new department.

THE EXPORT BUSINESS PLAN

INTRODUCTION

The export business plan, together with the associated financial business plan, is without doubt the most important document that you need to produce. It will enable you to control, direct and successfully manage your export programme.

This chapter outlines the major constituents of a strategic business plan for exporting. It also provides an introductory overview of some of the matters which need to be reviewed and included in a financial export plan. The strategic financial plan is usually produced as a separate document, and attached as a scheduled addendum to the strategic export plan.

Time spent in professional planning is never wasted. A well prepared, professionally documented export business plan will not only save you a great deal of time during the implementation phase, but also help to lessen the likelihood of incurring unplanned expenditure through the need to 'back-track' on your implementation programme, and to undertake additional tasks which were not included in the original planning process.

To take a rather extreme example, if you have not properly qualified your lead product against the competition in your intended market and arrive in-country to implement your programme, you may well find that much of your time and money has been wasted if your major competitor has cornered the market and is well entrenched with a strongly committed multi-level distribution chain already in place.

If you are already an experienced founding director, you may find it useful to review the first strategic business plan you produced (however long ago that was) – even if it is not relevant to your current business. Spending a few minutes doing so reminds you of the changes which have taken place since the original business plan was prepared. In almost every case we have reviewed, the current status and nature of a business differ considerably from the original strategic business plan.

It almost goes without saying that we have assumed that you have already qualified your product or service for its general export potential. Similarly, your products or services must meet legal, moral, safety and quality standards, as well as being culturally and socially acceptable, in your intended market.

Your initial basic market research should have qualified the general level of opportunity for your lead product or service. If you have any doubts about any aspect of this, you should spend additional time and effort on market qualification processes to ensure market/country compliance and general product or service acceptability.

We also must assume that you have already determined your financial budget, and have made provision for the costs of your export programme. If your programme requires additional outside financial investment (particularly if you are a small company), you must ensure that the funding is in place, agreed and available for instant use.

EXPORT BUSINESS PLAN: FIRST DRAFT

We now proceed to outline the development of the first draft of your export business plan.

It has been our experience that the simpler the export plan, the easier it is to implement. (Although simple, it can be fully comprehensive.) In practice, you need to qualify, document and strategically plan a relatively small number of fairly straightforward issues.

PRE-PLANNING ISSUES: INFORMATION NEEDS

The first stage in drafting a strategic business plan is the pre-planning stage, when you must consolidate your information. The issues to be included are listed in the form of a 'general considerations' checklist.

General considerations

1 a **You need to have qualified your product or service for its *general* export capability in its intended market, and to have evaluated its *saleability* and general profit potentials.** ☐

  b **You also need to have conducted comprehensive market research into the targeted geographic market and sized it, and have a high level of confidence not only that a market opportunity exists for your product or service, but that the targeted market has the capability of profitable commercial exploitation and relatively rapid short- to medium-term expansion.** ☐

2 **You need to know what production changes are required, and any costs associated with modifications or upgrades to your product or service which may be required to sell the product or service in the targeted market.** ☐

3 You need to know what additional internal/external training will be required to support the export programme and to have a firm estimate of the costs involved. You also need to have established an outline training programme plan and determined overall training time scales. ☐

4 You need to have carried out a 'fitness to export' internal programme and listed, and costed, any additional requirements which were highlighted as a result of this exercise. ☐

5 You need to have identified 'key players' in management, administration, production, finance, sales and marketing, not forgetting any specialist staff who may be involved in such areas as standards and quality control. You should also have prepared a new staff reporting structure for the export programme, and produced a first draft defining additional job responsibilities and job specifications. ☐

6 You need to have created, indexed, and refined an initial 'information base' relating to all aspects of the market which you intend to address. This should contain every single identified commercial contact name and address, telephone number, telex and fax number, together with any additional information on their operation you have been able to acquire. You need also to have produced a 'target' prospect list of potential buyers and/or interested parties. ☐

7 You should also have collected information about, and created a contact list covering: your own in-country embassy; any local government or other official contacts; import/export or trade associations; the local chamber of commerce; Customs & Excise/import regulatory bodies etc. ☐

The information outlined in the above checklist is very valuable to you, even at this stage, and should be considered strictly confidential. The value and worth of this information and contact list will grow considerably as your programme develops, and under no circumstances should 'free' access be given to this database. Staff access to this database should only be provided on a 'need to know' basis – and if you are very prudent on a fully restricted 'read only' basis. You cannot be too careful about data security. There have been too many incidents of information, including strategic plans, being leaked, or the poaching of staff, for you to be at all complacent.

SALES STRATEGY

The second stage of the strategic export business plan involves deciding how you are going to take your product or service to the market, that is, how you are going to sell it. At this stage you need to think strategically, not within closely defined operational parameters, nor at the detailed methodology. The major distribution and sale options open to you are as follows.

1 Direct sale by your own company sales staff into the targeted market.
2 Through the appointment of sales agents.
3 Through an appointed third party distributor network.
4 Through 'sell on' to an importer or wholesaler with their own in-country sales and distribution chain.
5 Through sales developed and promoted by a strategic business partnership arrangement or in conjunction with a joint venture partner.
6 Through in-country mail order (if the product is suitable for this distribution method).
7 Through an 'indirect' or independent sales organization which will take on your product and sell it through their own sales people. (This is a form of distributor sales.)
8 Through retail distribution, either yours or someone else's.
9 Through an in-country specialist who acts on a commission, and/or a retainer basis. This again is a type of agent sale, and is particularly suited to some market sectors with long lead times such as major high technology products, civil engineering projects and military products.

Remember at this time that you must think strategically. What may first appear to be the most cost-effective method of initial market entry, that which will produce early sales and revenue, may not be the best method in the medium to long term. Take a close look at the changes which have taken place in your home market sales strategy over the past five years. If you compare your current sales plan with that devised five years ago, you will immediately recognize many of these changes and acknowledge the reasons behind the change in tactics.

You should not consider entering into any immediate long-term contracts for the sale and/marketing of your products in your targeted country. On face value, a long-term sales and distribution agreement, well presented to you, may seem extremely attractive. However, in reality it can (and in the majority of cases does) hinder further market exploitation and major sales expansion.

An initial distribution or sales contract, regardless of the type of contract, should be for an absolute maximum of two years. The best option is a contract for 12 months, subject to review on progress to date. Do not compromise yourself with one totally committed distribution option before you start, no matter how good a proposition it looks. *Keep your contract time scale options open.*

■ Example

There is a very well-known UK company in the international military market sector which is still having to pay an 'introductory' commission to their original agent some 15 years after changing to another in-country distributor. This is the result of a long-term contract signed under some pressure in the early days of market entry from which they subsequently found that it was almost impossible for them to withdraw.

STRATEGIC LONG-TERM PLANNING

From a strategic viewpoint you must endeavour to plan for all reasonably foreseeable eventualities. However well your export business seems to be developing, you should always be aware of the possibility of an unexpected challenge by a competitor. If you are to maximize your opportunities, you need to engage in some lateral thinking.

Assuming you are not an opportunist exporter (and there are quite a number of these, some very well respected and totally ethical, who make a very good living in international markets – remember the Hula Hoop and all the more recent 'Star Wars' based toys), now is the time to strategically plan for longer-term market development, and to include these outline forward plans in your strategic business plan. Remember your strategic business plan is your route map for business development – not just this year, or next year, but forward for at least the next five to seven years.

In order to give you an insight into lateral thought processes related to strategic long term planning for exporting, consider the following example.

■ Example

During the 1980s a US-based company, which produces a relatively small range of personal computers, desperately wanted to expand its sales into the emerging and highly lucrative Middle East markets. Through a 'think tank' approach they recognized that there was excellent potential for a rapid response and highly customer service orientated company to achieve sales, but as the multinationals had already begun to become established there, they had many and (quite justifiable) reservations about attempting market entry in the face of this strong competition.

They tried to formulate a method of market entry which would facilitate market entry better, faster and more cost effectively than the already entrenched major players. They did not wish to become perceived as a major threat to them, and thus become involved in discount price wars, or similar such financially tough market protection practices, particularly during the second or third year of operation, when they anticipated a more substantial and faster growing market share.

Their market entry programme was intentionally fairly low key, but they did a number of things rather differently than others currently active in that market. To start with, instead of bringing in expatriate technical staff, they recruited and trained local nationals as sales support staff. This strategy paid dividends, in helping to persuade potential customers at 'sales and application' demonstrations of the benefits of purchasing their equipment.

Secondly, they set up a fast response engineering service organization. Because of their relatively small product range, their engineers were able to carry additional service/repair 'loan units' in the car with them. If the engineer was unable immediately to repair a faulty unit, they supplied an 'instant' loan machine – which generated a very high degree of customer satisfaction.

In addition, they set up a VDU, keyboard, and telephone cleaning service, which generated a considerable number of sales leads. They also introduced a very low cost 'Introduction to Personal Computers' course at their office – which was overwhelmed with local applicants within two weeks of announcement.

They also set up a computer supplies operation, initially for the supply of toner and film for their laser printers, but they quickly branched out into high quality heavier-weight paper, with a range of personal gifts to go with them, together with a good general range of computer supplies. Shortly afterwards they entered the emerging PC internal modem market, offering free installation and a free operator training course to support this new product. They did sell some modem boards and software.

Back in the USA they had about a hundred written-off ex-rental PC units. These were cleaned up, serviced and sent out by low-cost sea transport. They then used these units to set up a highly professional PC training school, and during the following year had over one thousand people through the course. What a wonderful way to promote your own product benefits and secure customer brand loyalty!

Needless to say, this company now enjoys a very prominent position in the PC market in the Middle East.

The above example demonstrates the benefits of thinking laterally and of strategic long-term planning, right from the start of an export market entry programme. If you think ahead and try to plan for comprehensive follow-on business development programmes – supported by quality sales promotion initiatives – this will always assist you to further develop your market share and secure additional revenues.

■ Example

A similar example is that of a UK exporter who manufactures paint, and exports his product to a European market. In addition to the direct sales of paint, he now has a complete range of painting and decorating accessories, comprising of brushes, tools, etc., together with a franchised hire business for steam wallpaper stripping machines and paint spraying equipment.

So, stop at this point and write a list of everything you can possibly think of as being complementary to your core product or service. List, in particular, any add-on or 'added value' products or subsidiary offerings that you could possibly include, and do not forget to include any new products or variations on a theme which you have already on your drawing board. Take time to plan for long-term vertical complementary product integration. The more opportunities you cover at this stage in terms of forward thinking, the greater will be your opportunities for further market development in the future.

STRATEGIC FINANCIAL PLAN FOR EXPORTING

You will remember that in the Introduction, we stressed in no uncertain terms the importance of the potential impact of your export programme on your home generated profits. Therefore, before we move on to consider the issues to be included in a financial export plan, we are going to examine in further detail some of the major financial implications of exporting.

You will already have an understanding of the importance of keeping close and accurate control of all costs associated with an export programme, of reconciling export costs and overheads regularly, and of regularly evaluating, comparing and measuring them against your home market financial status, profitability and cash flow. Before you undertake any further detailed financial planning, you should confirm your export financial investment decision, and secure the support and approval of your fellow directors/shareholders for the subsequent financial control and exposure limitation process. We have already (in Chapter 2) stressed the importance of calculating, at an early stage, your financial exposure ceiling. This is the sum which you will not exceed, under any circumstances, whether to attempt to retrieve accrued losses by additional investment, or to endeavour to recover accumulated losses already incurred through previous cash injections. This is not a defeatist approach, but a practical one, for if you exceed your ceiling, your home market profits will be severely affected. It is all too easy, especially if things are not progressing to plan, to enthusiastically 'bend' the budgets, or to inject additional (but totally unscheduled) capital into the programme, in the hope that everything will come right at some time in the future.

As a general recommendation, we recommend that your export programme cost exposure should not exceed one-third of your estimated net profits from your home market in any one financial year. (Calculating your export exposure limit may require you to make some assumptions about home market profit projections.)

Expanding into exporting is a major strategic business decision, on a par with other expansions, such as the construction of a new factory, an acquisition or a major investment in a new product.

You must make a strong commitment to your exposure limit. Experience has shown that companies that exceed their ceiling make no real achievements in terms of market penetration and that ultimately they have to write off their accumulated losses against home market generated profits.

If you ever find yourself in this position, it will be due not only to exceeding your exposure limit, but also to a fundamental planning error or assumption in your export planning process. The introduction of substantial extra capital, a major cash flow injection or even investment in large numbers of additional staff has very rarely succeeded in turning this type of situation around in the short term.

■ Example

A very recent example is that of a European trading company of high repute which entered the communications market in Eastern Europe. From the start they encountered a wide variety of business problems, including incompetent management and excessive expenses. After two years they realized that the overall project was so far behind financial expectations that very radical steps were needed – if a total write-off was to be avoided. At this point they were over budget by US$5m.

The company was virtually non-saleable and the only viable alternative to immediate closure and a massive loss was to invest heavily in a turn-round 'rescue' operation. Major investments had to be made to improve (i.e. completely redesign) the technological base of the company ($2m) and new executive management was recruited. Other necessary investments brought the total investment to nearly $9m. The original business plan and the original financial plan were now quite irrelevant.

The outcome of this débâcle was that they now had a saleable company, valued at about $5m, and an increasing monthly revenue stream. The 'pay-back' period estimate had been trebled, and the treasury funding had become some four times the size of the original 'investment' opportunity calculation. This additional treasury funding has had to be continued to support the 'developing' business and appears likely to have to continue for the foreseeable future – if they wish to capture additional market share.

This company will make a full recovery in due time – and even perhaps show a marginal profit – but what would have happened if:

1 They had had to use high cost external finance to support this project?

2 They had not been able to provide long-term support from their own treasury?

3 They had not had a corporate 'cushion' behind them?

There would have been no alternative than immediate closure and a massive write off.

If you had to face a similar situation to that in the above example, could you afford to do so? When you place your financial stake in the ground, stay with it. To do otherwise is just too expensive, too time consuming and too cash demanding, and does nothing for your company's long-term prosperity.

We will examine potential financial exposures again in Chapter 11, where we address some of the more complex financial controls and export budget questions.

We set out below a contents checklist for the first draft of your export business plan – see Chapter 7 for full details.

Export business plan (first draft): contents checklist

1 Introduction to exporting: why you need to export. ☐

2 A brief review of your products and/or services which are capable of being exported and your preferred lead product. ☐

3 A review of the changes and impacts an export programme will have on your current company, including training requirements and costs. ☐

4 Your potential markets: where they are, which is the best market geographically, and why. ☐

5 Competitive review of your potential market. ☐

6 Recommended and qualified selected method of market entry: review of alternatives. ☐

7 Outline marketing and sales support programme; advertising, sales promotion plans and an overview of your product launch/announcement programme. ☐

8 Sales and business development programmes. ☐

9 Technical support requirements plus any required repairs, spares and returns programmes. ☐

10 Strategic export financial plan: summary of costs and budgets. ☐

11 Complete market entry programme time scales and a calendar of events. ☐

12 Potential exposures: inhibiting and enhancing factors. ☐

13 General recommendation and summary. ☐

As we proceed through the following chapters, we will expand upon many of the topics covered above. Thus, it is important for your planning process that the full contents of each chapter should be read and digested before you start to generate any of the business plan items listed above.

REVIEW AND PREPARATION FOR MARKET ENTRY

INTRODUCTION

The preceding chapters cover a wide range of topics associated with many of the preparatory issues, widely recognized problems and genuine concerns related to overseas market entry.

In Part 2, we focus more closely on specific items of export market entry programme planning, in particular providing a very detailed review of strategic business plans for exporting. In Part 3 we examine and evaluate many of the alternative sales and marketing options for further developing your export market opportunities.

It is appropriate therefore, at the end of Part 1, to review some of the major topics covered so far, to enable you to further consolidate your thoughts regarding your exporting aims and objectives.

In real practical terms, the only real measure of success in export market penetration and overseas business development is sales achieved and direct profit generation. This comment appears throughout this book, in a number of guises so that you will fully appreciate the importance of this topic. Exporters may talk about percentages of market penetration, produce detailed charts evaluating competitive market share, or statistical or mathematical models of their complete market entry programme, but, in the end, it is the sales that count.

We now review the checklists presented in the previous chapters and provide an overview of the programme time scale options. From these options you will be able to select the most suitable method of export market entry – which is best suited to your own company, taking into account size and capability, and the specific range of goods, products or services you wish to promote in export markets.

REVIEW OF ACTIVITIES AND ACTION POINTS

Potential exposures

The ramifications, and potential exposures created through an undisciplined, uncoordinated approach to export market entry have been clearly outlined. Do not treat these comments lightly, or undervalue them. The examples provided are real, the consequences and various outcomes have been comprehensively documented for you (many are also in the public domain through extensive media coverage), and all have been fully evaluated for accuracy and relevance before inclusio[n] book.

Integrity of intent to export

Be absolutely sure of the true intent behind your wish to enter export markets. Qualify your intent through the personal review in the executive briefing in Chapter 2. Always ensure that your decision to effect export market entry is based on additional profit generation and increased sales, and never on personal aspirations or ambitions.   (*Chapter 2*)

Home market profit and market share optimization

Take a very close look at your current operation in terms of additional or further potential profit generation capability, before you consider implementing an export programme. It is always more cost effective to implement and control profit maximization programmes in home markets than in overseas environments. It can be confidently asserted that there is no company which has totally exploited its home market profit and market share potentials.   (*Chapter 1*)

Readiness to export

Using the 'readiness to export' evaluation programme described in Chapter 3, undertake a close scrutiny of your current business. Try to identify all the changes or upgrades necessary in order to enter export markets.

For some manufacturing companies, particularly those with fully automated production facilities, the changes that would be necessary could have a profound effect upon the decision to export – especially if the additional manufacturing costs involved would completely negate the projected export profit potentials.   (*Chapter 3*)

Training

Staff training requirements must be addressed early. The lead time for some parts of the staff training programme, such as export documentation and export financial instruments, are lengthy and need to be incorporated very early in the export training programme. (*Chapter 4*)

The executive briefing

A first class executive briefing goes a long way to smoothing the process of export programme acceptance. Pay close attention to the motivational factors, and ensure professional presentation at all times. Maintain export programme continuity and thrust by regularly communicating to your fellow directors and staff on programme developments as they take place. *(Chapter 2)*

Integrity of information base

Before preparing your first draft export plan, ensure that your export programme database is as good as you can possibly make it, and that you have all the current and relevant information to hand. This is vital in areas of potential market evaluation and competitive analysis. Your new contact list must be kept secure at all times, and regularly updated and expanded as new information becomes available. *(Chapter 5)*

'In extremis' financial commitment

Totally commit yourself to the 'ultimate exposure' financial calculation, and do not let anyone, under any circumstances, persuade you to change it. If you do, you are almost certainly placing your current home market business at a considerable and unjustifiable risk, and furthermore, taking an undesirable and unnecessary gamble with your company's short- to medium-term financial stability. *(Chapter 5)*

The export business plan

Take time and care with the preparation of your strategic business plan for exporting. Cover every topic listed, although some may appear to be rather lengthy and time consuming. We consider that each of these items should be included in a professional export business plan. *(Chapter 5)*

Integrity of financial estimates

Conduct a rigorous financial and budgetary evaluation. Ensure that all 'estimates' are truly representative and accurate. Insist on an itemized qualification process if you are all doubtful of data source, accuracy or interpretation. Check thoroughly, as you cannot afford not to get this most important process as accurate as possible.

Be especially aware of 'optimistic' sales forecasts, estimates of in-country operating expenses and any special one-off high cost items such as certification or licensing processes. As a quick fiscal check, run a spread sheet which reduces the sales projections by 30 per cent and increases the overall operating expenses by 25 per cent. If this projection destroys cash flow, profit projections, and draft P & L, you should re-examine all of the previously calculated budget and cost projections and re-evaluate them under stricter of terms of reference.

In simple terms, requalify and recalculate the budgets, and impose stricter cost and operating expense control limits. The above formula – although basic – very often reveals the true position. If you had proceeded on the initial financial projections, you would soon have discovered during the initial implementation phase their inaccuracy.

(Chapter 5)

Export budgets and costs

Ensure from the outset that a totally separate budget and cost system is implemented to control and monitor the export programme, and that everything, right down to initial research costs, is included.

Do not be afraid to reappraise and/or to restructure budgets as you proceed with your export plan – provided that you always ensure that you come in under the total target budget for the whole overseas business programme. Savings may be effected in some budget areas and marginal overspend accommodated in others. Exporting is not always strictly controllable, and you must be prepared for some financial 'surprises'. Thus, always try to ensure that your contingency budget is sufficient to support some unscheduled or totally unexpected expenditures. (As a broad rule of thumb, we would retain a minimum of 15 per cent in the unallocated contingency budget to ensure a reasonably safe margin.)   *(Chapter 2)*

PREPARATION FOR MARKET ENTRY

Having completed the review, we now turn our attention to more detailed preparation for export market entry.

The key to successful export market entry lies in the professional preparation and implementation of the strategic export business plan – in all of its aspects. We consider this to be so important that we devote the whole of Part 2 to its preparation and completion.

If you are going to succeed in global export markets you must have 'world-class' planning routines. Attention to detail and in-depth qualification processes are mandatory.

THREE BASIC OPTIONS FOR MARKET ENTRY

To enable you to start some initial time scale and calendar planning, we provide below approximate time scales for the different phases of various export market entry programmes. We have consolidated the wide variety of export market entry options into three basic programme types, which we term Programmes A, B and C.

These programmes range from a simple, single product market entry into one nearby country, right through to a multi-market, multi-product approach. You may wish to combine two of these options to better address the requirements of your specific product range or offering. In principle, there is no objection to combining two programmes into one – provided that you always use the operational guidelines, costs and time scales associated with the 'upper' level of market entry as your control factor. To try and compress a major programme – either by reducing the time scale, or by using a much shorter implementation programme – is inviting disaster. There are no known or recognized short cuts! Even an expensive public relations and advertising programme cannot by itself accelerate your market entry ahead of the limitations imposed by the basic market entry programme. Furthermore, the injection of additional money does not ensure the success of a project.

Programme A

Programme A is a basic export market entry programme – with one product or a very small product group, which is targeted to effect export market entry to one nearby country. This market entry is to be realized through the appointment of an in-country agent or distributor. The total time needed for Programme A is one year.

1 *Basic research and planning (3 months)*
   The basic research and planning stage includes market evaluation, product evaluation, competitive review, the 'fitness' programme, and the internal training review.

2 *Strategic business plan (3 months)*
   The strategic business plan stage should include all internal and external approval processes, financial provisions, complete programme documentation with associated time scales, and a comprehensive financial business plan. It also includes internal programme presentation and budgetary approvals.

3 *Market entry (3 months)*

The market entry phase includes the search for, selection, qualification and appointment of a single agent or distributor; the initiation of the physical exporting of the product by provision of samples/ demonstration units; any market 'launch' or advertising/promotion activities, and the setting up of initial management controls and agent/distributor reporting structures.

4 *Market consolidation (3 months)*

The market consolidation phase covers the business development programme, the closing of first orders and first order processing. It should also include the development of initial 'target setting' routines with the appointed agent or distributor, and future sales/marketing programme definition and costing in order to achieve additional market penetration. It also includes a complete and comprehensive agent/distributor performance review at the end of twelve months. (This ties in with our recommendation in Chapter 5 that you should not confirm an agent or distributor contract of more than one year initially.)

The above outline shows why it is necessary, even for a relatively simple export market entry programme, to allow at least one year to effect a professional entry. A reasonably large company with good internal resources might be able to compress the first three phases of the above programme into six months. Market consolidation, of course, does not begin until you are physically distributing your products, goods, or services in your chosen market.

We would normally recommend the above programme to small- to medium-sized companies which have not previously exported, and/or wish to initiate a low-cost, low-risk export programme to test-trial or to effect a low-key entry to new overseas markets with their products, goods or services, in order to gain overseas experience through a predetermined 'learning curve' process.

Programme A offers an excellent route to overseas market penetration for companies which have limited financial and staff resources. It also provides a method of export market entry which is considered to be relatively financially safe and secure and free from any major operational risks. In addition, the Programme A market entry option provides an excellent platform for companies which seek to 'trial' a small but closely defined export programme, before committing to an already agreed and approved major overseas initiative.

Programme B

Programme B is a more powerful and comprehensive version than Programme A. It is suitable for an operation which has a larger range of products or offerings, sold through multiple agents and distributors in one overseas country, and which is looking towards, in due course, the direct employment of its own resident in-country sales staff.

The time needed for Programme B varies between 18 and 24 months. This variation is due to the range of activities required to appoint agents or distributors (the number of whom is not fixed), and to cover an extended product range. The basis of the 18 months projection is for the appointment of one main agent or distributor, and up to four additional sub-agents, or a total of not more than six independent agents or distributors.

As product sets/ranges can vary enormously, from 300 different sizes of screws and fasteners (i.e., variations on one product set) to 300 separate stand-alone products, it is not possible to set precise time scales: however the requirement can be roughly calculated by averaging the time scale required for one product over the total number of products to be incorporated.

1 Basic research and planning (4–6 months)

It is essential for a company with a more comprehensive product range to examine the targeted market in more detail. This will take additional time, in direct proportion to the range and extent of the offering(s) proposed. However, as in most cases the additional products or offerings are complementary to, and within a similar market sector to the prime offering, a great deal of the market research may usually be combined, without any detrimental effects.

2 Strategic business plan (3–4 months)

The strategic business plan should include all recommended internal and external approval processes, financial provisions, complete programme documentation with associated time scales, and a comprehensive financial business plan. It should also include internal programme presentation, financial and budgetary approvals.

As the major constituents of the strategic business plan are the same as for Programme A, it should not take much longer to include additional information on extra product offerings. The financial business plan will need additional fields to cover the extra products, and closer detail needs to be paid to budgets, as the costs start to escalate quite dramatically with multiple product offerings, especially PR and advertising budgets.

3 Market entry (5–8 months)

The market entry phase includes the search for, selection, qualification and appointment of a number of agents or distributors; the initiation of the physical exporting of the product by provision of samples/demonstration units to multiple third party outlets; the agent/distributor product training programme; any market 'launch' or advertising and sales promotion programmes required for the group of products (plus possibly a 'corporate umbrella' programme); and the setting up of initial management controls and agent/distributor reporting structures.

Depending on the proposed agent/distributor structure it may also be necessary to develop management, control and co-ordination routines from main agent down to sub-agents or distributors. These are vital if you are to have any direct control over sub-agents or other secondary third party distributors.

4 Market consolidation (6 months)

The market consolidation stage covers the multi-layer business development programme; closing of first orders and first order processing to multiple distribution channels; the development of initial 'target setting' with the appointed main agent or distributor; and any additional sales/marketing programme definitions and costings to achieve additional market penetration within a multi-level market approach.

During the market consolidation stage you should also seek additional agents and distributors as back-up to your core distribution arrangements. With the very best of intentions and most careful selection procedures for agents and distributors, it is very likely that some of your initial appointments will not live up to mutual expectations and will have to be terminated in year two, possibly even in as short a time as six months if there are serious operational or financial (non-payment) problems with specific distributor or sub-agent appointments.

If you are astute, you will also keep a weather eye out for a possible main agent or main distributor replacement. Experience has shown that it is quite often the principal agent or distributor who must be replaced if any real progress is to be made with the sales and marketing programme.

Towards the end of the 18–24 month period you should have begun to assess the viability of setting up your own local sales structure. You should allocate time for this evaluation before second-year annual review with the main agent or distributor. For the reasons given above in relation to Programme A, we are very reluctant to approve main agents for longer than an initial two-year contract period.

Programme C

Programme C is appropriate for any export programme which includes large multiple product or service offerings into three (or more) countries through a diverse range of sales outlets, supported by a company's own 'in-country' management, administration, technical and sales functions. The time scale for Programme C is three years.

1 Basic research and planning (9 months)

A company with a comprehensive product range and requiring a multi-country entry within a defined and predetermined time scale must follow Programme C.

Entry to several countries should be phased, to allow for separate preparation for each. All the normal export market entry research and planning procedures are required for each country. As there is unlikely to be much common ground between countries, little duplication is possible with research – except perhaps in the formats used in evaluation and reporting – so each country has to be considered as a new export venture, requiring three months planning.

Inherent in this form of market entry are the 'people problems' associated with supporting new expatriate home country staff, or newly appointed local nationals. All of them will require new operating procedures, new forms of control, direction, plus a great deal of focused management time and attention. Do not underestimate these problems (and the associated additional time required).

Strict attention should also be paid to the logistics of redeploying staff overseas especially with the provision of accommodation, transport and health care.

2 Strategic business plan (6 months)

The strategic business plan should include all internal and external approval processes, financial provisions, and complete programme documentation for each targeted country, with associated time scales. It should also include a comprehensive financial business plan, individually analyzed by country, with a fully consolidated set of budgets and financial projections for the whole project.

The major constituents of this strategic business plan will take considerably more time to compile than the plans outlined for Programmes A and B, with the inclusion of information on the additional countries, and the incorporation of the size, shape, structure and costs of the various in-country management structures. The financial business plan will need extra fields to cover the additional countries, and separate country sections relating to office or factory premises, general overheads and administrative set-up costs. These costs cannot be 'averaged' from country to country, even though the set-up procedures and requirements may be very similar.

3 Market entry (9 months)

Ideally, it takes a minimum of six months for each country to effect a professional market entry. However, careful planning should permit some overlap. The problems of long time scales are greatly reduced by the initial inclusion of third party agents or distributors. In most major export programmes it is more time and cost effective to opt for a combination market entry programme from the outset, utilizing both agents and distributors and direct sales for securing and expanding initial markets.

As this topic is covered in greater detail in Chapter 17 we will conclude with the comment that it is far better to achieve professional, cost-effective market entry, with sustainable growth, in one or a maximum of two countries – than to find yourself with major problems in six!

4 Market consolidation (12 months)

It is in market consolidation that multi-market entry economies may be made. In many cases the business development, motivation, management control and direction procedures may be implemented across the board, with only minor modifications to meet special local needs.

Market entry time scale: summary

As you will appreciate from the wide variety of combinations of product mix, market sector, country and sales distribution arrangements reviewed above, it is almost impossible to be precise as to the time scale required to effect professional entry to any new export market.

Even with the best resources and financial and administrative support, export market entry always seems to take longer than the original plan, so it is wise to add a 20 per cent contingency factor. However, if your calculations indicate an implementation time scale varying by more than 20 per cent from our programmes, we recommend that you re-examine the accuracy and content of your strategic plan. Provided that you have incorporated all the recommendations of this book, your estimates should be fairly accurate. Nevertheless, even a few minor changes, modifications, additions, and/or variations will have a knock-on effect which can seriously affect overall time scales.

If you wish to make modifications, we recommend that you invest in activity planning software which incorporates a comprehensive range of bar-charts and flow-line diagrams, together with an imbedded time scale evaluation. At the very least, this will indicate all the major activity overlap or critical points which will require further in-depth review if you wish to prevent and overcome any manor 'multi-tasking' problems.

A final word of caution regarding time planning: regardless of any software, or additional staff support, do not try to complete too many activities at the same time. The control factors get out of hand very quickly, particularly if a number of different, and remote geographical locations are involved.

It is always preferable to include in an export market entry programme an implementation flow chart in the form of individual activity bars, detailing each separate activity, its location, duration, and time scale position, within the overall calendar of events. This will greatly assist both you and your staff in implementing your programme. It will also provide everyone involved with a common approach and understanding which will overcome many of the problems inherent in any multi-location, multi-tasking implementation programme.

The above activity analysis makes it easy to recognize points of high or concentrated activity, and any possible conflict of resources or staff availability. By intelligent manipulation of the positioning of individual activities and subsidiary programmes, it is usually possible to bring a few activities forward by a couple of weeks, or to delay the start of a new activity by a few days – which will give you a little breathing space to ensure professional follow-through, timely implementation and most important of all: a quality result.

CONCLUSION

Professional export market entry is really more a matter of the intelligent application of good commercial common sense than anything else. There is no mystique or exceptional skills required for successful exporting, with the exception of those in some specialist areas (already discussed), such as export documentation, financial instruments and customs regulations.

Part 2

THE EXPORT
BUSINESS PLAN
AND EXPORT
FINANCIAL PLAN

CREATING A STRATEGIC BUSINESS PLAN FOR EXPORTING

It is said that people who know where they are going generally get there. Never is this more true than with the creation of a strategic business plan for export markets. Approach the creation of your new export business plan with optimism, confidence and commitment, but take care not to become dogmatic. Over-planning is almost as detrimental as severe under-planning – they both generally lead to varying degrees of poor performance or outright failure.

EXPORT PLAN DEFINITION

Many of the export business plans we have reviewed are almost carbon copies of home market business development programmes. However, although the basic concepts and planning principles have a great deal in common, the content of home and export plans is very different.

Sound practice in a home market may be inapplicable and inappropriate in an export market. For example, you will almost certainly be faced with totally new distribution challenges, the degree of direct operational control will not match that in your home market, and you will also have to face problems of 'long-distance' management control of third parties and the motivation of agents/distributors. Further complicating factors include global time differences, and significant variations in attitudes, cultures and business practices.

SETTING OBJECTIVES

Every business plan, project or venture should have predetermined, well-defined, focused objectives. Let us look first at objective setting in general, and attempt to qualify this subject further.

A sound objective is always:

- focused and specific
- measurable
- realistic
- within a defined time frame
- easily and simply defined.

An objective is: *something towards which efforts are directed.*

In formulating your business plan, you must firmly define and qualify all of your export market entry objectives. All your objectives must be correlated within a predetermined market entry time scale.

When you set out to draft business objectives for your business plan, commence by noting the five criteria at the top of each page. Take time to think through your own specific export objectives in detail, as your plan will be focused directly towards achieving them. As you list your objectives, weigh each of them against the above criteria. Be critical and practical in your judgements.

In export review meetings, many people make general statements of the type: 'I want to sell my products in . . . '. They do not identify which products, nor state specifically where they want to sell them, what time scales are applied, or how the business programme will be measured.

If they had said: 'We wish to sell 500 units of the XYZ product in X country during the next twelve months', this statement – although by no means a perfect definition of composite objective – is far better qualified than the original statement.

Every company has different objectives – depending on their product and market sector, budgets, resources and time scales. However, there are some objectives which should be included in all well produced overseas business plans. These key objectives are:

1 **Sales volumes expected – analyzed by unit, value and margin.**

2 **Specific geographic area to be covered.**

3 **Time scale for each element.**

4 **Measurement routines.**

For any product, in any market sector, if you have closely defined these four factors, you are well on the way to successful objective setting.

POSITIONING YOUR MARKET ENTRY

Almost all new exporters would like to move as quickly as possible to the advanced market entry programme – Programme C – as described in Chapter 6.

Programme C is a complex multi-product, multi-market, multi-country overseas market entry programme. To achieve this level of market entry demands high skill levels from many of your staff, and a great deal of commitment, time and effort from many areas of your company – and substantial funding.

But is this level of market entry practical and realistic for you at your present stage of export development? Do you have the experience, expertise and resources to take on such a programme? For most international business developers, the answer is: No.

Even in some of the largest companies, one or more of these factors will be missing, so it is essential to decide upon a market entry position which is reasonably achievable in the short to medium term.

Companies which have already begun a planned programme of export market entry, and found it more difficult than they envisaged, should slow down until they achieve a positive result. Nevertheless, we do not condone under-targeting of objectives. If you have carefully qualified your internal capability to proceed with a higher-level market entry programme from the outset, do so with confidence. You will then be at least one year ahead in your export market expansion programme.

In the light of the above statement, now is the time to finally re-evaluate and to requalify your export objectives and to confirm, and commit them in writing in your draft export business plan. The major parameters of your capabilities to export, against which you need to set a time scale are set out in the following checklist. The questions which you will need to examine in order to conclude this section are as follows.

Capability to export

1 **Do we have a product(s) qualified as capable of sale in export markets?** ☐

2 **Do we have the internal resources to develop and support an export programme?** ☐

3 **Do we have adequate financial resources or export budget approved and available?** ☐

4 **Do we have the management skills and time to support this export programme?** ☐

5 **Have we identified and qualified the best target market?** ☐

6 **Do we know the resident competition and have we completed the competitive assessment?** ☐

7 Have we determined our best market entry method and distribution chain? ☐

8 Have we completed all the necessary in-country research? ☐

9 Have we developed a comprehensive database of information? ☐

If your answer to all of the checklist questions is 'Yes', you are in a very strong position to complete your export programme objectives list and qualify your market entry positioning. If you answered 'Yes' to seven of the questions, you should commence at the basic market entry level. If you answered 'Yes' to five or fewer questions, you should not commence an overseas business development programme until you have rectified the areas in which your capabilities are inadequate.

We recommend that you now return to Chapter 6 and qualify your responses to the checklist questions against the export programmes A, B and C. It should be fairly easy to qualify your own results, as the simplified programme types contain stages against which to match your responses to the above questions. Then record your results. If you are unsure of the accuracy of some of your responses, implement the next lower market entry programme.

The basic introductory level approach to export market entry provided by Programme A is the preferred route for almost everyone.

You will recall that in Chapter 6 we suggest times for each stage of the export market entry programmes. We hope that you will be persuaded by our experience that these times are realistic, reasonable and, above all, practical and achievable.

You should now be able to set objectives for the following sections of your business plan.

1 Target product(s).

2 Target method of market entry.

3 Target country.

4 Time scale.

You are now in a position to examine the remaining elements of the business plan.

FURTHER ELEMENTS OF AN EXPORT BUSINESS PLAN

Standard elements

We list below a number of items for selective inclusion in the first draft of your strategic business plan for overseas business development. These are the standard items which should almost always be included in a comprehensive export business plan.

Standard elements for inclusion in the first draft of a business plan

1 **Introduction: why export?** ☐

2 **Review of current business position; business expansion opportunities; list options.** ☐

3 **Export objectives.** ☐

4 **Evaluation of potential impact of exporting on current business.** ☐

5 **Market research report: competitive analysis.** ☐

6 **Proposed export market(s).** ☐

7 **Method of market entry.** ☐

8 **Time scales.** ☐

9 **Costs and budgets.** ☐

10 **Inhibiting and enhancing factors.** ☐

11 **Preferred option.** ☐

12 **Conclusion.** ☐

Additional information elements

In order to develop your export business plan to second draft stage, a wide variety of additional and diverse exporting topics need to be covered in some detail, and a comprehensive database must be developed to underpin them within the plan.

The list below, on effecting market entry into the European markets from virtually any country in the world, gives some indication of the very extensive range of topics that may need to be reviewed. Although the information requirements listed are specific to European markets, they may be applied to almost all international markets, regardless of geographic location.

Additional topics to effect European market entry

1 Brochure review programme ☐

2 Product opportunity analysis ☐

3 Business programme planner ☐

4 Programme implementation bar chart ☐

5 Direct mail programme ☐

6 Market research report ☐

7 Agent/distributor selection ☐

8 European Economic Community information briefing ☐

9 European businesses contacts database ☐

10 Euromarkets: executive briefing ☐

11 European Community legal and financial information ☐

12 European logistics information ☐

13 European language translation requirements ☐

14 European brochure production and translation requirements ☐

15 New business generation programme ☐

16 Prospect evaluation programme ☐

17 Customer enquiry response programme ☐

18 Sales visit schedule ☐

19 European buyers contact database ☐

20 PC-based communications package for sales staff (email) ☐

21 Agent selection programme ☐

22 Business builder programme ☐

23 Direct sales and marketing programme ☐

24 European incorporation: limited company ☐

25 European incorporation: PLC ☐

26 Leads generation programme ☐

27 European agent/distributor directory ☐

28 European joint venture information ☐

29 European grants ☐

30 European bank and financial services ☐

31 European insurance information ☐

32 European legal requirements for exporters ☐

33 European procurement ☐

This checklist is by no means comprehensive or complete, but it does indicate the range of topics that must be reviewed. Of course, not all of the items are immediately required if you intend to commence your export business development at the level of Programme A, as outlined in Chapter 6. However, every item is pertinent and relevant to European market entry. Even a very basic export market entry programme requires brochures translated into the local language, especially if your products are designed for a mass market.

REFINING THE EXPORT BUSINESS PLAN

INTRODUCTION

This chapter expands upon many of the topics reviewed previously, which have already been incorporated into the first draft of your export business plan. You need to take a closer look at much of the additional evaluation which must be completed to further develop your export business plan into a world-class document. To assist you in this process, we provide in this chapter 19 profiling formats, for you to complete. These formats have been designed to facilitate detailed and comprehensive information recording and analysis. We begin with a detailed examination of your company's growth pattern to date, a more detailed evaluation of your products and historical markets, and additional information on margins, product support and marketing issues.

After the profiling formats, we provide a detailed section-by-section analysis of the second draft business plan. This incorporates much of the information from the product formats.

INTRODUCTION TO THE PROFILING FORMATS

This chapter provides 19 profiling formats, which cover company profile, markets and products. Completion of these profiles will greatly assist you to identify and precisely quantify your current and historical market(s) and associated product positioning. You will be able to further evaluate this information against your known and perceived export market requirements and then to directly relate this to the appropriate section in your new export business plan.

The historical trend analysis formats included will enable you to examine in some detail your home market historical trends and developments, and to establish some common factors which may be useful for inclusion within your export programme. If you have been successful in home sales and market expansion, there will have been a number of good reasons for this. You need to identify these reasons individually and examine their overall relevance to your export programme. You may well find that there may be an area of common ground between these markets, in terms of sales and marketing programmes.

A programme which has been successful in one country, if carefully modified to suit export market conditions, will generally always stand a better chance of success than a sales programme which is totally new and untried. There are many exceptions to this statement, so be very careful in making assumptions about 'common ground' and always cross-check against known or perceived export-market conditions or requirements – before including any home market business programmes in your new export business plan.

Nevertheless, if you have already achieved considerable success in home markets, you will immediately recognize that your home sales and marketing plans were very closely allied to your objectives. It is a truism, but if you have the appropriate plan matched against the correct objective – success is usually the outcome. Please remember that it is not only the setting of export market objectives that is important, but also the recognition and evaluation of your current capabilities against those export market objectives. Strive to secure a good balance between the plans and the objectives at all times. Practicality and realism go a long way to achieving this.

We now turn to the company profile and product formats which will facilitate further market analysis and will assist you to more closely qualify your product(s) for export markets. N.B: these formats contain strictly confidential information about your current company status, your market share, product planning and new product development, plus additional information on your future business plans. Ensure their safe-keeping at all times.

COMPANY PROFILE FORMATS

The company profile formats provide a means of comprehensively reviewing your current company in terms of product and market sector, qualification of your sales and marketing aims and objectives, and highlighting the key points which should be included in your export business plan.

These formats have been specifically designed to assist you to transfer all your data easily to your export market entry programme database. You will also be able to use these formats when you wish to incorporate part of this information into subsequent documents and appendices, for example, the export sales plan, the export marketing plan and the export new business generation programme.

Some of the formats are of a more conceptual nature, such as the product development and product life cycle analysis. These formats will enable you to review your current product development plans for possible incorporation in your export programme later. Completing them will enable you quickly to take advantage of any additional export market sales opportunities which may occur in the near to medium-term future.

PRODUCT AND MARKET ANALYSIS FORMATS

The information which you will detail in the product formats will allow you to profile your products closely against your intended market sector, and more particularly, to identify, qualify and closely match any third party distribution requirements. The product and market evaluation formats use a technique that qualifies against current home market history and trends, and examines and qualifies these answers against your targeted export market.

Before completing any of these profiles, you must make the final selection of your lead product for export. If your company produces a range of small interrelated products it may be necessary to consolidate these offerings into one collective product set. This will then be treated as a composite single product which you will be able to promote as your lead product in your export market. This consolidation will give added focus to your export marketing programme, will reduce advertising costs and will simplify implementation.

The profile formats contain all the information and prompts required to enable you to fully detail your lead product against your market. You need to examine very closely the development pattern of your lead product(s) in your home market over the past five years, as this development quite often holds the key to successful sales migration into export markets.

When completing the profiling formats, and thinking about your export business plan, you must endeavour to produce a very close match between your current method(s) of operation and your export plans, in order to minimize the problems of change and the costs incurred.

This part of the information-gathering and analysis process is very important, as not only does it qualify your current business in detail, but quite often it enables you to select additional export options, that could potentially have added value or additional sales potential in your intended overseas markets.

It is important to complete the formats and questionnaires as comprehensively as possible.

FORMAT 1

Top ten products

This format contains information relating to your current product range. Please list in the spaces below your top ten products. Try to place them in order of importance for your export market, with your chosen lead product as No. 1. If you have more than ten major products in your range, group like products together and record this information on continuation sheets.

Product number   *Product name/identity/type*

1   _____

2   _____

3   _____

4   _____

5   _____

6   _____

7   _____

8   _____

9   _____

10   _____

Please list any other products for future consideration:

_____

_____

_____

FORMAT 2

Lead product

This format provides further information on your preferred lead product for export. From this format you will qualify your lead product Needs, Features and Benefits (NFB) list and determine the overall suitability of your lead product for your chosen overseas market.

1 Which is your selected lead product for export? _____

_____

2 Why do you consider this product is your best lead product for export?

_____

_____

_____

3 If you did not have the product above, what would be your second choice as a lead product for export? _____

_____

4 Why choose this one? _____

_____

_____

_____

5 Do you have any other product which, if suitably modified, could be better than your chosen lead product for export? Please describe: _____

_____

_____

_____

FORMAT 3

Lead product history

This format records the history and development of your selected lead export product. It is used to examine historical product development, part of which may be suitable for inclusion in your product marketing plan for export market entry.

1 How long have you had this product? _____

2 When was it originally developed? _____

3 Where was it developed? _____

4 Who was responsible for development? _____

5 How was it developed or originated? _____

6 Do you anticipate any further product development or are any product modifications scheduled to take place? Yes/No

7 If yes, please describe any scheduled product developments with their associated or allocated time scales: _____

_____

_____

_____

8 Could it be further modified for export? Yes/No

9 How could this be done? _____

10 What costs would be involved? _____

11 Would it be cost-effective? _____

FORMAT 4

Lead product sales history

This format examines the sales history of your chosen lead product for export. Please pay particular attention to this format as it may provide a clue to rapid sales programme implementation in your new export market.

1 When was your lead product launched? _____

2 Where was it launched? _____

3 How was it sold? _____

4 Was it sold in just one country originally?   Yes/No

5 Was it sold throughout the country?   Yes/No

6 If no, why only in selected areas? _____

_____

7 How many states/counties/cities was it sold in? _____

8 Has it been sold internationally?   Yes/No

9 In which countries? _____

10 Why in these countries? _____

_____

11 What was the result or outcome? _____

_____

12 If the result was poor, what factors caused this? _____

_____

FORMAT 5

Sales trends or volumes

This format lists sales per annum for your lead product and indicates sales trends over the last five years (number of units sold and sales value in US$).

1 Unit sales volume this year   (Year 0) _____   Value US$ _____

(Year 0–1) _____   Value US$ _____

(Year 0–2) _____   Value US$ _____

(Year 0–3) _____   Value US$ _____

(Year 0–4) _____   Value US$ _____

Total sales last five years   (Units) _____   Value US$ _____

2 Taking the above total for the last five years, calculate the annual percentage increase/decrease in sales volumes over that time.

% increase/decrease p.a.   Yr. 0 __   Yr. 1 __   Yr. 2 __   Yr. 3 __   Yr. 4 __

3 Are there any significant uplifts/downs in the above?   Yes/No

4 If yes, what do you believe caused them? _____

_____

_____

_____

5 Within any year have there been any seasonal variations?   Yes/No

6 Please identify them _____

_____

_____

7 Would this be the same for your chosen export market?   Yes/No

8 Why? _____

_____

FORMAT 6

Product resilience evaluation

This format provides information and considerations relating to key aspects of product resilience, hardness and performance.

1 Have you ever experienced any problems with your lead product, either technical, quality, or reliability? Yes/No

2 If yes, please describe:_____

_____

_____

3 How did you overcome these problems? _____

_____

_____

4 Do you anticipate any similar problems in your export market? Yes/No

5 If yes, what problems do you expect?_____

_____

_____

6 Has your lead product been modified? Yes/No

7 If yes, please describe modifications, upgrades, etc:_____

_____

_____

8 Do you require further upgrades or modifications for your export market? Yes/No

9 If yes, what should these be? _____

_____

_____

FORMAT 7

Product development

This format provides information on lead product development and any additional product developments required for your export markets.

1 Is your lead product now completely developed?   Yes/No

2 Does it have further development capability?   Yes/No

3 If yes, please describe: _____

_____

_____

4 Would it be possible to incorporate these developments into a special product for export?   Yes/No

5 If yes, what would be required? _____

_____

_____

6 How much do you think this would cost?   US$ _____

7 How long do you think it would take? _____

8 If you did this, how many extra sales would it generate? _____

9 Would it then be better than known competition?   Yes/No

10 How and why? _____

_____

_____

11 Would it be really cost-effective?   Yes/No

101

FORMAT 8

....

Lead product cycle evaluation

When you enter an export market the last thing you would wish to discover is that your lead product is becoming out of date or is due for upgrade or replacement. This format examines your lead product cycle and confirms and determines life expectancy.

1 How many years do you expect this product to continue in its present format/configuration? _____ Years

2 When do you expect to replace this product? (_____) (Year)

3 What do you expect or anticipate to replace this product with? Please describe preferred option(s): _____

_____

_____

_____

4 Do you have the product cycle life predetermined for this product, that is, do you have a product life expectancy determined? Yes/No

5 If yes, how many months? Years?

6 Do you intend to repackage or remodel to extend the product life cycle of this lead product? Yes/No

7 If yes, when do you intend to do this?

This year? ☐   +1 ☐   +2 ☐   +3 ☐   +4 ☐   +5 ☐

8 How are you going to do this? _____

_____

_____

9 What do you expect this to cost? US$ _____

FORMAT 9

Home market evaluation (1)

This format provides information and analysis about your home market.

1 What is your major home market sector for your lead product? _____

_____

2 Are there any secondary market sectors?   Yes/No

3 Please describe: _____

_____

4 Is your home market for this product:
Expanding? Yes/No   Static? Yes/No   Declining? Yes/No

5 Why is this? _____

_____

6 Are there any new known or anticipated market sector factors likely to affect sales volumes?   Yes/No

7 If yes, please detail: _____

_____

8 What is your SIC code (Standard Industrial Classification Code)? _____

9 Is there an opportunity in your home market to exploit a complementary range of model(s) or products?   Yes/No

10 If yes, please describe these complementary product(s):_____

_____

11 Does a similar opportunity exist in your export market?   Yes/No

12 If yes, in which market sector in your export market?_____

_____

FORMAT 10

Historical and current market analysis

The questions in this format relate to the historical marketing profile of your lead product over the past five years. The information in this format relates to the past and present sale and distribution of your lead product in your home market. Please complete both columns.

1 When you launched this product did you:

		Now	Then
1	Sell/market the product by yourself?	Yes/No	Yes/No
2	Employ sales staff?	Yes/No	Yes/No
3	Use agents?	Yes/No	Yes/No
4	Use distributors?	Yes/No	Yes/No
5	Sell through retailers?	Yes/No	Yes/No
6	Sell through wholesalers?	Yes/No	Yes/No
7	Sell by other third party distribution?	Yes/No	Yes/No
8	Sell by joint venture or partnership?	Yes/No	Yes/No
9	Sell through a subsidiary company?	Yes/No	Yes/No
10	Sell by any other method(s)?	Yes/No	Yes/No

2 If yes, please describe:_____

_____

_____

_____

3 Which of the above (1–10) could apply to your export market? Please list:

_____

_____

_____

FORMAT 11

Analysis of sales outlets

This format examines in more detail your current first and second level sales outlets and qualifies the type of outlets which have traditionally been successful for you.

1 When you launched this product in your home market, what type(s) of outlet(s) did you sell it to/through? Please list:_____

_____

2 Has this changed over the past five years?   Yes/No

3 If yes, please list all the new outlets you now sell the product to: _____

_____

_____

4 Do you expect this to change in the future?   Yes/No

5 If yes, what changes are expected? _____

_____

_____

6 Are you currently involved in, or considering selling this product into a second level market, that is, to become a part of another company's product, or to become any type of sub-assembly, or to be incorporated in another company's product range?   Yes/No

7 If yes, in what way have you done this? _____

_____

_____

8 Could this be feasible in an export market?   Yes/No

9 If yes, please list these potential second level export market opportunities:

_____

_____

FORMAT 12

....

Export experience (1)

We are now going to relate your lead product more closely with international markets. This format will evaluate your international profile and review any previous export market experience.

1 Have you ever attempted to export this product to markets outside your domestic home market?   Yes/No
   If no, go on to Format 13. If yes, continue below.

2 Was the export drive for this product a success?   Yes/No

3 If yes, why was it successful? _____

   _____

   _____

4 If no, please give the main reasons why this lead product did not establish or enjoy sales success in international markets: _____

   _____

   _____

5 Please list all countries in which you have tried to sell this product: _____

   _____

   _____

6 If you failed to establish did you end up well over budget?   Yes/No

7 In which areas and why? _____

   _____

8 Did this affect your home market business?   Yes/No

9 In which areas and why? _____

   _____

FORMAT 13

Home market competitive profile (2)

Regardless of whether you operate in home or export markets, competition can always have a profound effect upon the outcome of your sales programmes. In this format we list major competitive factors.

1 Do you have any direct competition?   Yes/No

2 If yes, please list all your competitors: _____

    _____

3 Which is your No. 1 competitor and why? _____

    _____

4 What product advantages do they have? _____

    _____

5 Could you incorporate these in your own offering?   Yes/No

6 If yes, how and at what cost? _____

7 Would this be cost-effective?   Yes/No

8 Do you hold current competitive information?   Yes/No

9 If yes, does this include:
   - Competitive pricing information?   Yes/No
   - Competitive terms and conditions information?   Yes/No
   - Competitors' discount structures?   Yes/No
   - Competitors' installed base information?   Yes/No
   - Competitor technical information?   Yes/No
   - Competitive marketing information?   Yes/No

10 Do you know about competitors' new product development?   Yes/No

11 Could these developments affect your market share?   Yes/No

12 If yes, in what way? _____

    _____

FORMAT 14

....

Export market competitive profile and review (2)

This format lists major international competitive factors.

1 Do you have any direct international competition?   Yes/No

2 If yes, please list all known international competitors: _____

_____

3 Which is your No. 1 international competitor and why? _____

_____

4 Which is their major country(s) of export? _____

5 Do you have any other major international competitors?   Yes/No

6 In which countries? _____

7 What product advantages do the above competitors have? _____

_____

8 Could you incorporate these in your own offering(s)?   Yes/No

9 If yes, how and at what cost? _____

10 Would this be cost-effective?   Yes/No

11 Do you hold current international competitive information?   Yes/No

12 If yes, does this include:
   • International competitive pricing information?   Yes/No
   • International competitive terms and conditions information?   Yes/No
   • International competitors' discount structures?   Yes/No
   • International competitor installed base information?   Yes/No
   • International competitor technical information?   Yes/No
   • International competitor marketing information?   Yes/No

13 Do you hold information on international competitive new
   product(s) development?   Yes/No

14 Could these new developments affect your market share?   Yes/No

FORMAT 15

Product needs, features and benefits analysis

This format analyzes the key needs, features, and benefits (NFB) of your lead export product.

1   What is the major reason why a customer or company needs your product?_____

2   For what other reasons would they need it? _____

_____

3   Is it required or needed for a special or technical reason?   Yes/No

4   If yes, what are the specialist needs? _____

5   What type of person or organization needs this product? _____

6   Why?_____

7   Do you have an export prospect list of these companies?   Yes/No

8   If not, why not? _____

9   What are your major product features? _____

10   What are the minor product features? _____

11   Does your product have any recognizable poor features?   Yes/No

12   If yes, what are they?_____

13   Could you improve any feature(s)?   Yes/No

14   How and at what cost? _____

15   Does your lead product have one major single benefit?   Yes/No

16   If yes, please describe: _____

17   Will this key benefit apply to your intended export market?   Yes/No

18   What other benefits will apply to export markets?_____

_____

109

FORMAT 16

Margin analysis

One of the major points to consider when entering an export market is the management and control of product margins. This is especially important when your intended market is a great distance from your production facilities and substantial additional overheads for transportation and distribution are incurred. This format examines some of the questions relating to margin management and identifies key areas of concern.

1 Since this product was introduced has its percentage profit margin declined, remained the same, or increased? _____

2 If the margin has declined, what caused this decline? _____

_____

_____

3 Is your margin coming under competitive pricing pressure?   Yes/No

4 If yes, do you believe that repackaging or re-presentation would help?
                                                                      Yes/No

5 If yes, do you have any plans to do this?   Yes/No

6 If yes, when do you expect to do this?   Month _____   Year _____

7 Towards the end of the lead product life cycle do you intend to gracefully lower the price of the product to seek ultimate profit potential?   Yes/No

8 Would you be prepared to do this in an export market?   Yes/No

9 Is your lead product:
 • High margin product?   (over 50%)
 • Medium margin?   (30–50%)
 • Low margin?   (below 30%)

10 What is your expected margin on your export lead product? _____

11 How have you calculated this? _____

_____

_____

FORMAT 17

Pricing analysis

This format reviews major pricing issues.

1   Is your current pricing recognized as competitive?   Yes/No

2   If no, why not? _____

3   Do you regularly carry out pricing reviews?   Yes/No

4   Do you have a competitive price discount structure?   Yes/No

5   Do you move prices with competition?   Yes/No

6   What effect would a 10 % increase in price have on current sales of your
    lead product in your domestic market? _____

    _____

7   What effect would a 20 % price increase have? _____

8   If you reduced price by 10 % or 20 % would this increase sales? Yes/No
    • By what percentage for a 10 % reduction?   _____ %
    • By what percentage for a 20 % reduction?   _____ %

9   Could the margins realistically stand this?   Yes/No

10 Do you have any special offers?   Yes/No

11 Are they seasonal?   Yes/No

12 Do you have special government, medical or educational
    institution prices?   Yes/No

13 Do you have special staff purchase prices?   Yes/No

14 Is competitive pricing really an issue with your product(s)? Yes/No

15 If no, why not? _____

16 What pricing changes could you effect to double sales? _____

    _____

17 Have you ever tried this?   Yes/No

FORMAT 18

Resources and support analysis

This format examines resources – technical and/or engineering support in your home market – and examines the need for such requirements in your intended export market.

1 Does your lead product require any on-site support?   Yes/No

2 If yes, what type of support (technical, installation, administrative, specialist)?_____

3 How is this done in home markets? _____

4 How would you structure or provide this in an export market? _____

_____

5 How many home market field and site support staff do you have? _____

_____

6 What is the percentage ratio of support, installation, technical staff to sales?   _____ %

7 Would you require a similar ratio in an export market?   Yes/No

8 Do you need home market service, repair, maintenance staff?   Yes/No

9 Would you need this support in your export market?   Yes/No

10 How would you organize this in your export market? _____

_____

11 Do your technical support, installation, service staff require special qualifications or specialist skills?   Yes/No

12 If yes, please list: _____

_____

13 Do they need specialist tools or equipment?   Yes/No

14 Do these people need to have people or sales skills?   Yes/No

15 Do you have a recruitment profile for these people?   Yes/No

16 Are support staff readily available in your export area?   Yes/No

17 How do you normally recruit them in your home market? _____

_____

18 Will you be able to do the same in your export market?   Yes/No

FORMAT 19

Sales staff review

This format briefly reviews some additional sales issues.

1 How many sales staff do you have at present? _____

2 Do you expect to recruit any additional sales staff?   Yes/No

3 Do you intend to reduce sales staff?   Yes/No

4 What effect would a 20 % reduction in sales staff have? _____

_____

5 Do you know what your true sales staff costs are?   Yes/No

6 What is the average cost per sales person (home market)? US$ ____ p.a.

7 What is the average cost per sales person (export market)? US$ ____ p.a.

8 Do you know the home market norm cost for a sales person?   Yes/No

9 Do you pay: Above market norm? ☐   Average? ☐   Below norm? ☐

10 Do you have a sales commission or bonus scheme?   Yes/No

11 What is the ratio of salary to commission or bonus in percentage terms?
                                                         _____ %

12 Are your current sales staff happy with this scheme?   Yes/No

13 When did you last review, change or update this? _____

_____

14 Do you know your sales employment costs in your export area? Yes/No

15 If no, how are you going to find out? _____

_____

_____

16 Do you know your home sales expenses costs?   Yes/No

17 Do you know what they will be for your export area?   Yes/No

18 What percentage above home costs do you expect them to be? ____ %

19 Will your export sales staff require accommodation, cars or drivers etc.?
                                                                     Yes/No

20 Do you know what these costs are likely to be?   Yes/No

SUMMARY OF PROFILING FORMATS

Having completed all the profiling formats and the checklist on elements to be included in a business plan (*see* Chapter 7), you should now have a much better understanding of many of the additional issues which must be reviewed for your overseas business plan. Even if you are an experienced exporter, you should find that the profiling formats provide a useful cross-reference list of many of the additional and often unrecognized factors associated with exporting. We have never found a company that could complete all the questions without reference to other sources of information or making some estimates.

Each format contains specific information and questions relating to an individual exporting subject. Within your own 'world-class' export business plan, each of these subjects should be reviewed, in greater or lesser detail, according to your own product(s) or market sector requirements.

You will have appreciated, from the diverse range of questions within the formats, that it was not intended that your answers should become direct inputs into your export business plan. Rather, the questions have been designed to stimulate and encourage serious reflection about how you are going about your business now.

The basic elements of an export business plan should now be brought together, qualified and documented, as your second draft strategy for exporting. Accurate documentation is the first requirement.

PLANNING STRATEGY

We now consider planning strategy, since professional planning is vital to success. The more thoroughly you plan, the better your chances of succeeding.

A document may be termed a strategic plan, but unless it is properly structured and it is fully qualified, it is not a genuine strategic plan. If the planning process involves these three elements, the plan should develop correctly and the easier you will find it to qualify levels of export market opportunity, and to select the most appropriate methodology for overseas market entry.

So, let us look at the components required for the initial planning process, rather than the plan itself. The primary requirement for the process of planning is to establish, as we have stressed before, your aims and objectives.

The planning process should contain the following five phases.

1 The objectives, aims and mission ratification.

2 The information source clarification.

3 The scheming, discussion and theorizing process.

4 The qualification process.

5 The plan assembly process.

You will shortly be ready to undertake a second draft export plan, fully itemized and fully qualified. The qualification process is vital, as it is essential to ensure the best possible, up-to-date and accurate information.

Your first outline draft export business plan should contain the following sections (presented here in the form of a checklist).

Outline contents of draft export business plan

1 **Introduction, setting out the broad terms of reference and why we should consider this opportunity.** ☐

2 **The aims and objectives and a detailed description of the target market.** ☐

3 **Method of market entry.** ☐

4 **Costs and budgets.** ☐

5 **Time scales.** ☐

6 **Conclusion.** ☐

We now move on to include all of the additional information gained from the profiling formats within a second draft export business plan. You will appreciate that we are now working with 'hard' (that is, well qualified) information. It is at this point, within each key section of the business plan, that you should begin to concentrate in more detail on your own particular products and services, and address more specifically your individual market sector. We cover this process in more detail in Chapter 12.

STRATEGIC BUSINESS PLAN FOR EXPORT: SECOND DRAFT

Key points of plan contents

1 Introduction
  a Introduction to your field of exporting
  b Terms of reference
  c Why you should export
  d Outline of potential benefits

2 Aims and objectives
  a Business mission statement for exporting
  b Key five top objectives
  c Describe each of the five objectives

3 Potential market
  a Describe your potential and intended market
  b List countries you want to approach
  c Highlight estimated potentials in each country/area
  d Evaluate competition
  e Highlight growth capabilities

4 Selected method of market entry
  a Describe options
  b Qualify selected method
  c Detail selected method

5 Costs and budgets
  a Determine venture or start-up budget
  b Determine cost of sales budget
  c Year 1 – draft cost and budget projections
  d Outline cost budget for Years 2 and 3

6 Time scales

    a Determine overall time scale for market entry

    b Determine time scales for each part of the programme

    c Prepare action and time scale list of key areas by quarter/month

    d Prepare master time scale plan and bar chart implementation programme

7 Conclusion

    a Detail inhibiting and enhancing factors

    b Highlight any potential impact on current business

    c Your specific recommendation

    d Thanks to participating staff for their help with the preparation of the export business plan

Appendix A Marketing report

    1 Marketing report on target market

    2 Information base

    3 Competitive review information

Appendix B Financial evaluation

    1 Export budgets

    2 Cost estimates

    3 Draft P & L for first two years

    4 Cash flow projections

BUSINESS MISSION STATEMENTS

INTRODUCTION

The subject of business mission statements is not extensive, but of sufficient importance to warrant separate treatment. A good business mission statement is an excellent business tool – if managed effectively.

Every company should have a business mission statement. It is a 'window' into your company, which can capture the interest of prospective customers. A good business mission statement provides confirmation of your purpose, your commitment to your enterprise and your professional approach. Many countries, particularly those in the Far East, place considerable importance upon business mission statements – much more so than many Western countries. This is partly cultural but it may well stem from the attention to business detail which prevails in many of these countries.

In this chapter we examine the constituent parts of a 'world-class' business mission statement (BMS), look at some of the options, and provide some general guidelines for preparing a BMS.

The first requirement of a BMS is that it must be concise. If it is too long it just becomes another sales promotion aid. It must be expressed in positive terms, without any general or grandiose statements. The three most important characteristics of a BMS are as follows:

1 It is a selling document.
2 It should identify your lead products and/or market sector.
3 It should contain your company name and logo.

REVIEW OF BUSINESS MISSION STATEMENTS

There are four essential areas which must be covered in a BMS for exporting. These are as follows.

1 An explanation of the specific task(s), product, goods or service.
2 The purpose, objectives and aims.
3 The commitment from the company to succeed.
4 An indication of the time scales for the above.

Time spent drafting and refining this mission statement is well spent. It is important also to ensure that your export BMS is compatible with your domestic BMS. Use your domestic BMS as the basis for your export BMS, taking into consideration the factors reviewed earlier in this chapter and the key points 1–4 listed above.

Later in this section we look at a combined mission statement, that is, an international BMS which reflects not only your home market capabilities but also your new capabilities in overseas markets. We recommend this as the best solution, since one mission statement can then be used in all situations.

We have, however, left the final judgement on this matter to you. Previous experience has shown us that, in some circumstances, it is advantageous to have dual business mission statements, especially when customers or prospects might perceive possible contention or conflict between domestic and international markets. Thus, we have allowed for three levels of mission statement.

Domestic business mission statement

Please detail below your current business mission statement.

_____

_____

_____

_____

_____

_____

_____

Export business mission statement

Please draft below your proposed export business mission statement.

_____

_____

_____

_____

_____

_____

_____

International business mission statement

Please draft below your proposed international business mission statement.

_____

_____

_____

_____

_____

_____

_____

Having now produced your first drafts of the different business mission statements, compare them with the characteristics and key points listed earlier in the chapter. In doing so, ask yourself these questions:

Review of BMS

1	**Is it a corporate selling document?**	Yes/No
2	**Does it describe, introduce and provide an overview of your main products?**	Yes/No
3	**Does it reinforce your company name and logo?**	Yes/No

We now present what we believe is a new idea, namely the incorporation in a strategic business plan for export of an internal 'financial business mission statement'.

Financial business mission statement

Your export initiative will normally only be judged as successful if it is proven to be financially advantageous to your company. The financial business plan underpins the strategic business plan with all the necessary cost and budget estimates, financial plans and forecasts, to enable you to succeed in this aim.

In order to focus more attention upon financial planning, we believe that it would be greatly to your advantage to complete a similar BMS exercise totally dedicated to financial aims and objectives.

This financial BMS must include the following key points.

1 The qualification of the financial task.
2 The purpose, aims and objectives of the financial BMS.
3 The committed and approved financial procedures and resources.
4 The finance review time scales and schedules.
5 Confirmation of your financial exposure limit calculations.

The above document should be referred to regularly at all formal financial review meetings. It will assist in reaffirming financial objectives and add considerable focus to reviews of current financial performance in your overseas markets.

QUALIFYING AND CONFIRMING EXPORT MARKET POTENTIAL

It is almost impossible to accurately 'size' a potential export market from a distance. This is one area of exporting knowledge which really does need a great deal of local information in order to assess true potential. So, how do we obtain all the necessary information?

As is often the case, the speed and accuracy of data and information acquisition is directly related to the amount of time, money and resources invested. The time required may be reduced by investing heavily in outside assistance, but that does not automatically ensure the quality and accuracy of the information gained.

THE OPTIONS

There are three major options open to you, each involving different degrees of cost, levels of complexity and different time scales.

Option 1: international marketing consultant

The most expensive option is to employ a reputable firm of international marketing consultants to undertake a comprehensive market survey and evaluation on your behalf. Provided you give them a good general briefing on your products, and closely define the market sector in which you wish to operate, you can usually leave the rest to them. However, there are some drawbacks.

1 Using consultants is usually very expensive. Even a minor market research project covering only two or three major points relating to market potential will usually cost over $10 000 (excluding business expenses). A more comprehensive market sizing and export product potential evaluation, complete with a competitive analysis and review and competitive market sector evaluation, could cost five times as much. However, the time scale is relatively short: most of the large international market research and market analysis companies will usually be able to complete an evaluation of one country within six to eight weeks.

2 Quite often, professional market analysts have to make a number of assumptions which are based on the best current market information

available in relation to the potential 'fit' of your products into that market. In almost all cases, the more closely, and more accurately, you brief your consultant (especially in relation to product type, product capabilities and product definition), the better will be the overall resulting report.

If you are going to invest a considerable amount of money in this form of consultancy based market research, do your own research first. Your consultant will need to know exactly the parameters of your programme, your target market, your perceived inhibiting and enhancing factors and will need a great deal of information about your aims, objectives, products, goods or services. A one page brief is insufficient. This is certainly one situation where best briefing input equals best report output.

3 As reports of this type are prepared for a fee, considerable attention is paid to final report presentation and the provision of background and supplementary information. Many of the 'presentational' aspects, such as visual aids – full colour pie charts, graphs, bar-charts, etc. – add very little to the content, and are very often quite difficult for non-marketing professionals to interpret. Your briefing should state that a minimum of such elements are required, and that you are seeking specific 'hard' information, not readily available general or background information.

Furthermore, there is no guarantee that any consultant will make the correct analysis. There are many factors to be taken into consideration when evaluating new market potentials. For example it is easy to make a wrong competitive assessment. It is almost impossible to get to know the plans of a major competitor – who may be, for example, about to introduce a major new product line.

The other methods of market potential evaluation involve a greater degree of self-help, perhaps with some professional assistance in the acquisition and interpretation of information.

Option 2: a planned co-operative programme

The second option is a planned programme in conjunction with your chamber of commerce, department of trade, a world trade centre, or a government export promotion department.

Option 3: a self-generated programme

The third option is a self-generated package which entails visits to your target market and evaluations carried out by yourself or your own staff.

For most potential exporters who are operating on limited budgets, Option 2 offers the best value for money, and is more cost-effective than Option 3. Option 3 often entails a number of visits to the targeted country of export, together with all the associated costs for air fares, hotels, transport, and translators/interpreters etc. We therefore focus on Option 2 and provide you with a basic operating and research plan to secure the desired information.

DEVELOPING GOOD RELATIONSHIPS WITH INFORMATION PROVIDERS

As we pointed out in Chapter 1, there are many sources of good quality and mainly free information, which is readily available to any potential exporter if only they take the time and trouble to seek it out.

Chambers of commerce

Membership of your local chamber of commerce, in addition to providing you with services, information and contacts in your own country, can provide you with an introduction to the chamber of commerce in your target country. Membership of that chamber provides you with valuable information on such matters as local trading conditions and market sectors – information not easily obtainable in your home country. Membership also provides you with local contacts and personal introductions to the local business community. You may find that good connections with the local importing community will also often produce excellent results.

Trade information through embassies

Many countries have export promotion programmes supported by the commercial departments of their embassies around the world. You are usually asked to contribute a modest sum to offset any expenses incurred. We have seen some excellent local reports compiled at very modest cost by embassy commercial sections which have proved invaluable in market evaluation and analysis. However, the staff of commercial departments do not welcome requests for free, and in-depth market evaluations on behalf of a single company. You are advised to participate in an existing and established embassy programme.

If you enter an embassy programme in a courteous and businesslike manner, you will very often end up making good friends with the 'in-country' commercial department staff, and quite often they will provide you with additional local export trade information. Of course you must never offer private consultancy fees to embassy staff. This is strictly forbidden, and often regarded as highly insulting by the staff, and any such offer would damage the reputation of your company.

If you can find an 'inside track' commercially, that is acceptable, but do not try to involve government employees in dubious tactics or monetary inducements. You will not only place their jobs at risk, you will inevitably also attract the attention of the embassy security staff.

Your embassy, high commission or trade legation in your target export country is your friend and mentor. Never forget to call upon them when you visit the country. Not only is this a business courtesy, but it is a special opportunity to establish your company's presence, and to promote your export programme on a more personal level.

A quick final note regarding in-country embassy contacts. From a personal security viewpoint it is always worth your while to register your presence as soon after your arrival as possible, with the embassy chief security officer, so that, in the event of a major accident, serious illness or even worse, they know you are in the country, approximately where you are, and have a record of your company and next of kin details.

Departments of trade and industry

In many countries departments of trade and industry, at national, regional or state government level, co-ordinate, and assist with, a wide range of export activities. You should find out how they can assist you with export market information and market penetration programmes. For example, they may offer central government sponsored support to international trade shows, exhibitions, seminars and overseas trade missions. They may have a special department to support export initiatives.

Other information providers

There is one further source of information, which many potential exporters overlook – the embassy, high commission or trade legation of your targeted country within your own country.

ADDITIONAL MARKET POTENTIAL EVALUATION

The basic information requirements for market evaluation are of six types. These requirements are of general application and are not product specific or market sector dependent.

1 Quantifying the size of the potential market.

2 Determining its geographical location.

3 Establishing the maturity of the market.

4 Compiling information on the competition.

5 Determining the expansion potential.

6 Reviewing levels of cultural, religious and economic acceptance.

If you have information in broad terms on the above points you are well placed to make initial decisions about market potential. Remember that all data should if possible be obtained and verified at source, that is, in the intended country of export. Under no circumstances should you include in your export database information which is based upon 'averaged' sales or 'estimated' market penetration in your home country.

■ Example

A very good example is provided by the sales of wallpaper. For example, from published national statistics from trade organizations in the USA and Germany, it is fairly simple to determine an average volume for the national consumption of this type of product in those two countries. If you refine this information into specific geographic sectors, or identify areas where high-cost wallpaper sells well, or where cheaper types are preferred, you begin to gain an understanding of sizing and geographic distribution issues.

If you try, however, to transfer these averages to a Middle Eastern country or perhaps to Pakistan, your statistical analysis is totally worthless.

Let us now take a closer look at the individual base information requirements listed above.

Potential market sizing

In order to 'size' the potential market you need information on a number of points.

1 What is the average annual consumption or purchase volume of the product?
2 Is it an expanding or 'buoyant' market?
3 Is the market a new market, a 'traditional' market or a strictly 'entrepreneurial' market?
4 Is it a declining market?

Geographical location

One of the basic rules of successful exporting is to take your product first to a closely qualified, defined and targeted geographical market within a larger market. This provides the best opportunity of rapid product establishment and the generation of local sales. This 'local' establishment and consolidation may then be rapidly expanded to cover the whole country or geographic region. In some countries, for some products, the potential market may be only the capital city, for other products, it may be rural areas or industrial areas, while for some lucky entrepreneurs, the market extends to every single member of the population.

Make a critical examination of your product, and try to be as objective as possible in assessing the likely level of acceptance in your intended market. Use your information base to qualify population density, quality of location and geographic location.

If your product is population density sensitive, seek out the major conurbations rather than attempt to cover the whole country. This will focus your efforts and resources into closely defined geographic areas, and make the best use of your sales development and sales promotion budgets.

Information is generally available on 'quality' of residential areas in almost all countries. If in doubt ring the local embassy direct, as they will almost certainly have this information. Information on industrial locations is also usually readily available, often with a composite listing of resident companies together with their industry codes, names of contacts, telephone, fax and telex numbers. If the targeted country has a *Yellow*

Pages or a similar publication, obtain a copy. Assess any distribution difficulties if you intend working across a wide geographic region. If transporting goods up-country adds 30 per cent to the price, you must be confident that you have a real chance of being competitive against local offerings.

It is all too easy to appoint a remote agent when you are aiming for wide coverage: they are probably eager for additional product lines. However you must be very sure that you can really afford all the time and effort needed to train, equip, monitor and control them, and that you can afford to supply additional demonstration units or samples to capitalize on the opportunities. Think very hard before you decide to go countrywide.

Market maturity

Judging market maturity is very difficult. How do you judge whether a product is viewed as a short-term gimmick or whether it has the capability of long-term lucrative market exploitation? To judge market maturity you need to know if the market is new, growing or in decline.

There are, however, some indicators. Obtain the best possible market information you can from the sources described previously. Look closely at the year by year import statistics for your product group and plot these on to a graph. Set up another graphical projection of the total estimated market available and compare the two lines. If the total available market is less than double current sales for the *sector* (by which we do not mean a *niche market*) the market is probably mature or going into decline. You should not pursue this market.

Be realistic in your evaluation and judgements about levels of market maturity. At the top end of your potential market there may be little opportunity, but at lower levels there may be excellent opportunities: do you remember the success with which low cost transistor radios were 'dumped' at the lower end of the US and European markets not so many years ago?

The competition

Probably the only good feature of competition is that at least it helps create market awareness. Nevertheless, however unwelcome, competition has to be faced in almost every export market you wish to enter.

The competition is usually of two types: resident 'in-country' competition, and other 'international' exporters selling into the same market.

Both have market share, and both want *more* market share. You have to break into this scene to sell your products successfully. The more you know about your competitors, the better placed you will be to achieve this. Companies rarely truly know their competition in depth. (The retail food market sector is a possible exception.)

Resident 'in-country' competition

Resident competitors in your targeted export country represent perhaps your greatest overall competitive risk, as they will be able to respond more quickly, and at far less cost, than you, or any other international exporters.

You should undertake a comprehensive review of local competition on your first visit to your target market. Visit as many outlets as possible that could stock and sell your product(s) and see just exactly what is on offer. If your product is of a specialized nature, seek out the local trade association and obtain a members' list, obtain catalogues and brochures, buy or subscribe to local trade magazines and journals, and always seek to acquire all of the competitive technical specifications that you can find. Compile all of this information into a competitive activity file, listing and detailing each potential competitor separately, and remember to update the file regularly. Out-of-date competitive information is worse than no information at all, as you may be led into making false assumptions with outdated data. Try to develop a common format for recording competitive information, using the same fields of information in each file, and in chronological order. This will greatly facilitate comparisons and other competitive evaluations.

If you appoint an agent or distributor, the appointment agreement should specify that the agent or distributor is required to gather and forward to the principal's home country head office all major competitive information, plus media comment or other information upon your product or market sector.

Other 'export' competition

Finding out about international competition is a little more difficult, as your competitors may be widely scattered throughout the world. Perhaps in this case, the most economical and the fastest way to obtain additional information is by the 'indirect route' of an expressed third party purchase interest.

If your major competition has its own public share issue you should buy a few shares to hold privately. In this way, you will be entitled to receive the information prepared for shareholders. In addition to the published accounts (which quite often detail export results separately), you will quite often be sent corporate publications which describe in great detail all of the company's activities, the year's accomplishments and plans for the future. Information prepared for shareholders almost always contains highly useful competitive information, which is freely and legally available to anyone who makes a small investment in their shares.

MARKET EXPANSION POTENTIAL

The expansion potential of your target market is of two types. The first is the expansion potential of the market for the products that you are launching into the market. The second is the lateral market expansion capability, which refers to the market for complementary products to your lead product set, but still within the same general product sector. (Remember the paint manufacturer who expanded his business into decorators' supplies etc.) If you are trying to assess market expansion capability, first examine the market size, and then look at its maturity. These are usually good indicators of expansion potential.

CULTURAL AND ECONOMIC ACCEPTANCE

It is essential to ensure that your products and everything associated with them – packaging, advertising, brochures (including content, style, colour, etc.) – are culturally and economically acceptable. You must be alert to the cultural and economic differences between your target market and your home country. For example, the colour white has a special meaning in some parts of the world: in some places it is associated with death. The best way to ensure cultural compliance is to seek the advice of a well-educated resident national. Perhaps the greatest sensitivity transgressions occur with printed brochures. Check these for cultural or religious sensitivity. Brochures or similar advertising materials which may be regarded as a little roguish (but reasonably acceptable in the western world) may shock or greatly antagonize people in other cultures.

Economic sensitivity

If you are considering entering a market where economic factors play an important part in the buying decision-making process, pay close attention to the relative 'economic worth' of your product and to its pricing. If the per capita national income averages less than US$20 per month you will have problems if your $10 product is one with mass market rather than niche market appeal. People need to eat before they make any non-essential purchases. You may have the best product in the world, but if it is beyond the purchasing capacity of your main consumer market, because of its price, you will not sell very many. Obviously, there are exceptions to this rule, and there are, for example, quite a number of Rolls Royce cars sold into niche markets all over the world. Your best guide to matters of economic sensitivity is common sense, based upon good quality local research.

GEOGRAPHIC ANALYSIS

How do you decide which countries you should target for your export programme? It is sensible to start with a process of elimination.

There are a number of points to take into account as possible selection criteria. Some of the key items are listed below.

1 Distance from the home market: long-distance management and control problems.
2 Language and cultural difficulties.
3 Political and economic factors.
4 Established, mature or declining market conditions for your product sector.
5 Logistics and distribution problems.
6 Costs involved.
7 Specialist installation or technical support requirements which may be needed.
8 The customers' ability to pay for imported goods and services. (This is particularly relevant in the Third World.)
9 Are you allowed to sell your goods there? (This is of significance for high-tech products.)

10 Currency regulations and currency exchange problems.

11 High levels of competitive activity.

12 Economic stability.

To the above list you should add any specialist requirements necessary to support your product in an export market, regardless of geographic location. Also add any factors which you realize will affect, perhaps impede, sales of your product or service. Quite a number of the factors to be taken into consideration in the selection of an export market are not product or market sector dependent.

On the basis of industry knowledge, new commercial information, export briefings etc., you are now in a position to examine every country in which you think there may be an export market and qualify each against your selection criteria.

Ideally, you should try to select a market which is close to your home country, where your exporting overhead costs and management control problems are minimized, the logistics problems are relatively small, the market is expanding and there is relatively little competition.

First-time exporters should not be too ambitious. It is best at the beginning to try the easy route with a qualified 'near' market. A near known market may not be as large as you would wish, and there may be some entrenched resident competition, but at least you know a potential market exists, and because it is relatively close, it will not take a great deal of time, money and effort to secure professional market entry.

Many potential exporters divide the world into geographic 'target areas' – USA/Canada, Europe, Asia, Africa, the Middle East or the Pacific Rim countries. This approach is far too ambitious and fraught with problems. It is far better to select a single country, or better still a carefully qualified part of that selected country, and to strictly limit yourself to that geographic area until you are established. If you cannot effect successful export market entry under carefully calculated, appraised and controlled conditions into a carefully qualified, limited market, how will you fare trying to effect entry into a major global segment?

By undertaking a rigorous qualification of the potential markets you should by a process of elimination be able to reduce your list to no more than three good, solid and realistic possibilities.

You should now further pursue your 'in-depth' market research programme to obtain additional information on these three opportunities, with the ultimate intention of selecting a single country – with one carefully qualified back-up opportunity in case your additional research uncovers some serious inhibiting factors relating to your proposed entry into your prime targeted country.

Having now completed the geographic profiling exercise, and finally selected your best 'calculated' target market, you must now turn your attention to additional ways of evaluating your product or service against the target market opportunities. You have already covered a part of this exercise with the profiling formats provided in Chapter 8, which enabled you to take a close look at your products, market trends and historical home market development, and to undertake a brief Need, Feature and Benefit (NFB) analysis of your lead export product.

We now continue with a process by which you will be able to evaluate and measure your product potential in your targeted market. By its very nature this exercise must cover a wide range of topics, so, to save time, we offer a simplified version of this analysis, through which it should be possible to cover almost any product or service offering 'pre-qualified' as basically exportable. How do you measure market potential?

MEASURING TARGET PRODUCT POTENTIAL

The first question to ask is: What do we measure product potential against? You know that you have a good quality exportable product, but how will it perform in the targeted market? There is no certain answer, only some logical conclusions. Without the benefit of trial marketing you are, at the very best, forced to accept estimates based upon carefully researched information. You have already qualified some important points. These are presented in the form of a checklist.

Evaluating target product potential

1 You have a reasonable estimate of the total market size in terms of units sold per annum by competition (or imported), or a good estimate of the number of potential units that could be sold per annum in an expanding market. ☐

2 You have qualified the product for general in-country acceptability, and taken a close look at pricing and economic issues. ☐

3 You have carried out a comprehensive competitive evaluation and now know a reasonable amount about the performance of competitors' products in the targeted market. ☐

From the above, and the information obtained about the maturity of the targeted market, you should now be in a position to make some balanced judgements.

Perhaps the best way to explain how to measure product potential is to take an example of a single lead product introduced into a new export market, and follow it closely through each process of evaluation and analysis.

■ Measuring product potential

Let us assume that you wish to enter France with an electric drill manufactured in the United Kingdom and suitable for the do-it-yourself market. You have qualified your potential outlets as major DIY stores, the leading high street retailer chain stores and a mail order catalogue. You have also identified some additional market opportunities (as yet unqualified) selling to garages, maintenance areas, low volume production facilities, carpenters, 'fixers' and installers, the electrical installation industry, plumbers and communications system installers.

You know from market research that throughout France this market is worth over one million francs per annum. The anticipated market will comprise replacement purchases for broken or worn-out drills, some first-time buyers and a smaller number of customers purchasing a second drill (perhaps an additional cordless, specialist or heavy duty drill).

There will also be an unknown number of DIY-type drills used (probably because DIY drills are cheaper than industrial models) in non-mainstream production, or in installation operations. This area will provide you with additional market opportunities.

The market is dominated by a resident French competitor, who has almost 40 per cent of the home market, the remaining market being shared by a German manufacturer (25 per cent), a Japanese manufacturer (20 per cent) and sundry other manufacturers taking the remaining 15 per cent. Using price lists and simple mathematics, you have been able to calculate an 'average' drill price across all manufacturers of 150 francs per unit. This calculation indicates that the average volume in terms of units sold per annum throughout the country is in the region of 6500 units.

From consulting trade publications, you have seen that sales of this type of product in France over the past five years have been increasing at a steady rate of approximately 300-500 units per annum. Thus, it is reasonable to assume that you are considering entering a continuing growth market which has not yet peaked. Table 10.1 sets out some of the statistics you have gathered from your in-country research.

Table 10.1 Market for drills in France

Model manufacturer	Market share (%)	Units sold p.a.	Value (FF)
Maxima (French)	40	2660	400 000
VerkElectrika GmbH (German)	25	1660	250 000
Speedeezy (Japanese)	20	1330	200 000
Remainder	15	1000	150 000
Total	100	6650	1 000 000

As the market is currently expanding at a rate of approximately 300 to 500 units per annum, let us err on the side of caution and use the lower figure of 300 on which to base further market expansion calculations. We will assume for the purposes of this exercise that your offering is going to be in a similar price range to the 'average' price per un t, and that it has similar features and functions.

The French market is clearly cominated by some entrenched 'local' and 'export' competition which has expanded to take up the total market currently available. There is also a new pctential market of some 300 additional units which could be sold into any of the above market shares. (On balance it is reasonable to assume that the resident French manufacturer will get the lion's share of this market.)

If you are going to enter this market and wish realistically to size your opportunity in terms of the potential number of units sold per annum, you have to make some additional calculations based on the level of difficulty required to take a section of market share from each of your resident competitors. Forgetting for a moment the additiona market expansion of the 300 new units per annum, let us concentrate on this po nt for the time being. To sell your product in this market you need to take market share from someone else. Who is it going to be?

Without any special features cr functions or price advantage it is going to be difficult to take a share cf this market away from its major incumbent – the French manufacturer. They already probably enjoy a reasonably high level of brand loyalty, have extensive distribution faci ities and outlets and almost certainly have a professional service and repair organization.

The first recommendation we would make is to look carefully at any additional features or functions cr added value items which could be added to, or incorporated in, your product at minimal cost to enhance your overall offering. The product could be further enhanced by means of some additional 'added value' special introductory offer extras, such as a cased set of drills, bench rest, or a drill depth indicator etc. to try tc promote initial sales.

However, without any additional product enhancements and with advertising support and in-store promotion aids similar to those of the resident competition, it should be possible to secure a foothold in this market. We would expect sales to be in the region of 3–5 per cent of the market in the first year, the lower figure being achievable without any substantial product enhancements, promotional or additional added value offerings. If you offer all the product enhancements from the beginning, you almost certainly will improve on 3 per cent, but, if things do not go well for you, what do you have left to offer? It is sometimes preferable to delay some of your offerings until you have had a chance to evaluate competitive reaction.

The 'soft underbelly' of this market lies with the minor market share occupied by the 'rest' of the competition, and you should target this specifically before you come into direct confrontation with major market share occupants. Remember the last thing you want on your hands at this moment is a major price war! The major market share is taken up by the resident French manufacturer, and they will find it far less painful than you would, substantially to reduce their selling price, as their overheads on distribution and direct cost of sales, including management costs, are usually considerably less than those of the 'export' competition.

If you enhance your product a little, and especially if you give some form of 'added value' to the product, you stand a good chance of improving your market share potential in the first year from 3–5 per cent, up to a realistic maximum of 7 per cent. Anything beyond this figure, in the first year of market entry, we would consider unrealistic given the market conditions outlined above.

Ideally, it would be prudent if you designed your marketing campaign to address the market sector currently occupied by the 'rest' of the competition. However, in reality, you should take some additional sales from all of the major competitors, albeit in small volumes. There are always some people who are willing to try a new product – especially if it is well packaged and presented, and more particularly if it exhibits demonstrable additional added value.

You are now in a position to try to evaluate this French market potential. It seems that you could achieve sales of between approximately 200 units (3 per cent of market share) and 450 units (7 per cent of market share), with the mean being between 300 and 350 units. You now need to evaluate profit potential against projected costs and budgets. This subject is covered in Chapter 11.

We hope that the above example, although rather basic, gives you a brief insight into the problems associated with trying to determine product potential in a new market. Companies very often fail to meet their sales targets in export markets simply because they try to relate their sales forecasts to projected costs, instead of the other way round.

Do not be over-ambitious in your first year of export market entry: do not expect to become an instant 'cash rich' company, do not expect to take the lion's share of the available market. Companies often have unrealistic sales expectations and make unrealistic projections, given the market conditions and the status of competition. Most companies in this position budget and cost against these unrealistic unit sales projections, thus unwittingly placing themselves in a serious loss position even before they start their formal market entry.

LEAD PRODUCT EVALUATION

If you are to sell any product in any market, whether home or export, it must be saleable. The above example shows the need for the customer or buyer to be able to perceive added value and/or product enhancement. If your product is to sell in volume, it must offer considerable actual and perceived benefits over comparable offerings; if you can also offer reasonable price competitiveness, you should have good results. A slightly higher price is acceptable, as long as you are able to fully justify, and prove this, in terms of features and functions, to a potential customer or buyer.

Finally, we must emphasize that high-priced, under-featured products, goods, or services of 'concealed' inferior quality have no place in global export markets. They may enjoy some initial success if promoted intensively but in general their success is very short lived.

It is salutary to consider the performance of the Far East and the Pacific Rim countries over the past few years, and the extent to which they go to package, present, enhance and add value to their products, with the result that in some sectors (such as television and hi-fi equipment) they dominate the world market.

The Japanese car industry has won a very considerable share of the international market in a relatively short period. Many of their early offerings were not of very high quality or reliability, nor were they generally perceived as offering very good value. Now, however, product enhancement and perceived added value have totally changed their image. Extra items are fitted as standard on almost all their vehicles, guarantees are generous, with two or even three years of extended warranty offered as part of the package and trade-in values are now generally good, and represent real value for money.

There is a great deal to be said for learning from your competitors – especially in product development and product enhancement. This is perhaps the most cost-effective method of developing a new product, or varying an old one, without all the additional R & D overheads associated with a total re-design or a new concept. Far Eastern companies do this very effectively.

FINANCIAL PROCEDURES, BUSINESS CONTROLS AND MANAGEMENT REVIEW PROCEDURES

INTRODUCTION

This chapter reviews all the major financial procedures, business controls and management review procedures necessary to effectively manage an overseas market entry business programme.

The information in this chapter is of particular relevance to small to medium-sized companies which do not employ their own finance professionals. However, as this chapter examines many of the *strategic* financial considerations and issues which should be included in any professionally produced overseas business plan, it is also directed at experienced finance professionals.

This chapter takes a practical approach to many of the problems associated with export finance, based on experience of 'realigning' export programmes or implementing overseas financial 'rectification' programmes. In particular, it addresses many of the problems associated with mis-matches between projected export sales volumes and the true cost of initiating, implementing and developing the export business.

This book does not include a detailed review, explanation or summary of financial instruments, methods of payment, export finance and export documentation or an overview of the more intricate details of overseas insurance requirements. This exclusion is deliberate. These subjects are adequately covered in readily available specialist publications relating to export documentation and procedures.

One important point with regard to published works of reference is that although the information they contain is excellent, in terms of quality, depth of knowledge and understanding of export documentation, legalities, information about export controls and procedures, etc., they very quickly become out of date. It is essential, therefore, to check – both at home and in the country of export – that your information is current. This is particularly important in relation to government import or export restrictions and conditions, customs and excise regulations, tariffs, taxes, duties, and other such matters. Most changes are issued without any warning, to avoid a 'run' before the changes are implemented. Uplifts in rates of duty are a classic example.

For example, if import duty has risen, and you have already contractually agreed a delivery price in your country of export (with no 'variation of duty or tariff' clause in your contract) you could suffer a loss even before your goods, products or services reach your intended market.

This example reinforces our earlier advice recommending specialist training, particularly in relation to export finance documentation.

We estimate that a qualified accountant will take at least three months (on a part-time basis) to learn the skills required to manage export market finance documentation effectively. Less senior, less experienced or less qualified staff will require longer.

THE FINANCIAL BUSINESS PLAN

We start our examination of a financial business plan by looking at some general topics and then extend and build upon these to draw up a comprehensive and professional plan.

We assume that the reader has a basic general knowledge of finance and general accounting practice, including a reasonable understanding of such fiscal matters as cost evaluations and budgets, cash flow, margin analysis, cost of sales, profit & loss projections, accounts receivable etc., and the composition of company accounts and balance sheets.

The key strategic financial considerations for exporters are as follows.

General financial considerations for exporters

1 The preparation of a strategic financial planning document.
2 A detailed export financial plan.
3 Risk analysis.
4 Export budgets.
5 Cost control.
6 Home market profit impact analysis.
7 Margin analysis.
8 Determination of a strategic 'fall-back' position.

FINANCIAL STRATEGIC PLANNING AND THE DETAILED EXPORT FINANCIAL PLAN

A dictionary definition of 'strategic' is: 'of great importance within an integrated whole or to a planned effect'. We focus here on the words 'integrated whole' and 'planned' within the context of an export finance plan.

We believe that the best way to commence any strategic business plan for exporting is to create a simple outline financial plan based upon cost centres. This will put into place the basic financial information under the appropriate headings, and will assist you to further qualify and develop your export budgets, financial limits, controls and procedures for your export market development programme. This document (after redrafts and revisions) will subsequently become your formal financial business plan in your strategic business plan for export. It will become 'of great importance within an integrated whole' and will underpin your export business plan in all respects.

We recommend that your strategic finance plan for export be spread initially over a three-year period. Even a relatively modest export market entry programme requires one year to effect market entry, the second year to consolidate that position, and the third year to further extend market share. Each one-year programme requires individual professional financial planning, if you are to avoid unexpected outcomes or financial exposures. The following discussion is based on a three-year strategic financial plan.

The first draft of your financial strategic plan for export should include the following items.

1 **Financial objectives and time scales.**

2 **Evaluation of potential financial exposures.**

3 **Outline costs and budgets.**

4 **Control and measurement procedures.**

5 **Contingency plans.**

You also need to have completed some basic financial research in order to determine some base line costs relating to your proposed lead product(s), anticipated margin(s) and some base information on transportation and distribution costs. This information is generated from home country product cost and margin information or can be obtained from commercial quotations.

Later in this chapter we will add further items to the above list to extend the scope of various topics, we will evaluate them in more detail and then will incorporate them into a coherent financial framework which is PC spreadsheet compatible.

Contingency planning is essential. You must have a defined and documented fall-back position to enable you to cope if your financial plans fall behind schedule or cost/revenue ratio expectations.

Poor or badly researched financial programme planning (especially in relation to budgets), or an 'unscheduled' major omission from your finance business plan, could have serious adverse effects upon your home market profitability. Be prudent, plan carefully and make sure that you generate a financial fall-back plan early in the planning process.

The checklists in this chapter, for both strategic items such as the calculation of 'fall-back' position, and comparatively less important tactical matters such as individual budgets, must be thoroughly reviewed – for both accuracy and content – before you complete your financial business plan for export.

FINANCIAL OBJECTIVES AND TIME SCALES

As already explained on the previous page, the strategic financial plan should be spread over three years and specific time scales must be stated for the various activities.

Risk factors

All exporters face major risks, as a result of which they may fail to achieve many of their objectives. Our experience leads us to make the following observations, which indicate the scale of the risks involved.

1 Over 90 per cent of exporters fail to meet their original sales projections.
2 Over 95 per cent of exporters fail to meet all of their original cost and budget objectives.
3 Over 60 per cent of exporters fail to meet their time-scale plan.
4 Over 60 per cent of exporters fail to meet their original market share projections within a three-year period.

As we have already stated, the major reason for the failure of so many companies to achieve their export ambitions is their inability to achieve their export sales targets.

It is a fairly easy procedure to 'revise' the product margins to endeavour to remain within a profitable programme – but, if the sales are not there, you will not have any margins to revise!

EVALUATION OF POTENTIAL FINANCIAL EXPOSURES

A very practical way to address the prime financial exposure of under-performance of sales is to evaluate, determine and qualify the export sales revenue expectations in close conjunction with sales and marketing departments. In reality, virtually all 'downstream' financial planning is geared to this. A major error of judgement at this stage will have considerable ramifications right through your financial planning process. However, if sales projection statistics are adequately and professionally qualified and verified and levels of reasonable expectation are thoroughly confirmed right at the commencement of your financial planning process, there should be little or no need for contingency plans.

The qualification of sales revenues, in terms of either $ revenue generation or units sold, is not a precise area. It is without doubt one of the most difficult areas of business to address professionally. It is subject to a considerable amount of estimation and the quality of sales forecasts is always subject to interpretation – right down to the level of individual order prospects.

Initial analysis

To conduct an initial analysis of the financial statistics you have already gathered or which have been provided, apply the following formula:

1 Take the first year's sales projections and reduce them by 29 per cent.

2 Take the total of your projected cost of sales (not venture set-up costs) and increase them by 34 per cent.

3 Take the first year business programme schedule and increase the time scale to 15 months. (Do not forget to extend the cost base accordingly.)

4 Deduct any 'venture' or initial set-up costs which have been included for recovery in Year 1.

Run the above analysis as a spreadsheet so that it will be easy to extend it to Years 2 and 3 if required.

We have applied the above formula to over one hundred market entry programmes across a very broad cross-section of the world's markets and have found that, with only a very few exceptions, our analysis has been within plus or minus 15 per cent of the final financial outcome.

We believe that this formula gives an excellent overall 'early warning' projection if applied to any strategic business plan for export prior to implementation. It should not be discounted purely on the grounds that it is very difficult to verify the applied percentages, or to quantify the methodology. We certainly know that it has proven consistently accurate across a wide range of product and market sectors and geographical locations, too often to be ignored.

If you apply this formula to your draft business plan sales and cost expectations, you will almost certainly see that the budgets are in disarray, the costs are escalating and you have an additional three months of programme implementation costs to include in the finance plan. You could now be facing a potential loss. The lesson to be learnt from this exercise is that, to make a profit from your export programme, you now need to prepare urgently a new financial business plan, addressing levels of sales expectations, budget and costs.

You need to look closely at restructuring the export overheads (not the export venture capital) and bring them into line with revised sales projections. Plan for a time-scale 'slippage' of between 20 per cent and 25 per cent per month, and downsize your market share expectations accordingly.

Any new business programme needs up-front venture finance. These costs should be reviewed separately and, as they are usually so high, should not be included in the financial plan as fully recoverable in Year 1. To try to recover them in the first year would damage an already fragile financial base. We recommend that you do not attempt to recover start-up costs until at least the beginning of Year 2 of market entry.

Financial benchmarks

Your financial strategic business plan should always include a series of financial benchmarks or reference points by which to measure and judge progress to date. If progress is measured in terms of sales achieved and any further or additional budget release is qualified against an accurate forward sales forecast on a monthly or quarterly basis (depending upon the product or market sector), this will give you sound financial control. If sales fall seriously behind forecast, undertake an immediate review. If you fail to do so, the situation will almost certainly deteriorate by the time of the next scheduled review, which could be at least three months away. Act and respond quickly – it will save money. Sales and marketing departments are likely to object to such strict financial control. However, it is essential that you stand firm, so that you do not lose financial control at this point. Firmly remind them that everyone committed to the agreed business plan and agreed to a financial benchmark approach.

You will recall that the strategic business plan included the following items.

1 The sales promotion and marketing budget flow will be directly related to revenues generated from units sold.

2 Any additional budget release will be geared to sales achieved and only released against a very certain and sure forward qualified sales forecast.

Calculation of fall-back position

As we stated in Chapter 2, and have continued to emphasize, it is very important to determine your ultimate fall-back position in relation to your total export venture capital limit. This is the sum beyond which you will not seek to attract further investment in your export programme. This figure indicates the extent of risk you are willing to take in exporting. The fall-back calculation should also take into account the level at which any accumulated losses accrued from an export programme will begin to affect your home market profits, either generating serious cash flow problems or imposing unacceptable cumulative losses upon your overall business. You should always first secure your core business – and safeguard it. If you fail to do this you may well lose reserves, a situation from which it will take you a considerable time to recover.

COSTS AND BUDGETS

Before you start preparing cost projections and budgets, you should separate all of your financial reporting and statistical analysis for your export market entry programme from your main company finances. If you do not do this, you will never have any true reconciliation of your overall export programme costs. You will be unable to determine true overseas operating costs or profitability; nor will you be able to exert any really meaningful financial controls.

We recommend that, in addition to the normal standard cost and budget centres which you use on a day to day basis, you should include the items in the following checklist in your export budget. Remember, you cannot control what you do not measure.

Export budget cost centres

1   Export programme start-up costs (the export venture budget). ☐

2   Research and information base development costs. ☐

3   All travel – both within the home market for research and overseas visits. ☐

4   Dedicated export secretarial and administration costs. ☐

5   Export training costs, including export sales training. ☐

6   Export marketing and advertising costs. ☐

7   Any translation or additional export contract legal costs. ☐

8   Costs of membership of export organizations, chambers of commerce etc. ☐

9   Dedicated or additional export staff costs. ☐

10 A proportion of corporate overhead costs. ☐

Without a checklist, it is all too easy to omit a vital item. A classic example of a budgetary 'omission' for exporting is the non-provision of a budget for samples and/or demonstration equipment. To provide even a modest range of samples or demonstration units to as few as 20 potential outlets adds up to a considerable budget item. Added to the cost of providing these are costs for transportation, customs duties, packaging, sales and technical literature, translations, technical support or specialist sales training, transit insurance, etc. The addition of all these costs could almost double the cost of your initial launch budget estimate.

CONTROL AND MEASUREMENT PROCEDURES

We discussed earlier in this chapter the need for appropriate benchmarks and measurement routines to be inserted at key points in the export business programme in order to effectively measure progress. We now examine this topic more closely and look in more detail at how to achieve this.

The standard financial measurement routines and controls for your export programme are not very different from those normally used to financially control and evaluate home markets. The export financial controls use almost the same fiscal disciplines as your home market, use similar but separate cost centres and almost certainly will be programmed to run on the same computer. Even in the smallest company, a reasonably configured PC is quite capable of running all the required data and financial analysis outlined within this book.

We now look at how we monitor export finances, and how we measure the current financial status of the export programme against the objectives detailed in the export business plan.

The general principles behind the following recommendations are that we must always know what our true costs are, how and where they have been accrued, in which cost or budget centre they should reside, and that we must have an easy means of regularly reconciling these overheads against export revenues generated without recourse to extensive additional financial management routines.

We recommend that for the first year at least, the export programme is fully audited on a monthly basis, and that a direct comparison is made against the objectives detailed in the business plan. We further recommend that quarterly benchmarks be inserted into the finance plan which (when achieved) trigger release of the next quarter's budget allocation.

It is far better at this stage to control the allocation of budget funds in this way than to allow access to the whole of the first year's budget from the beginning, only to find in Month 7 or 8 that all of the budget has already been spent. Regardless of the pleas from marketing, sales and other areas, key additional budget release to revenue achievement, and do not be sidetracked into bending the rules if things are looking tough. Remember our earlier comments about additional (and/or unbudgeted) capital or budget injection if things are not going to plan. In nine times out of ten the situation does not improve, the losses only become greater.

FINANCIAL CONTINGENCY PLANS

As we explained earlier in this chapter (*see* p. 147) it is essential to have contingency plans, with a well thought out fall-back position. We recommend that you create two financial contingency plans, Plan A and Plan B.

Plan A

Plan A is a fall-back plan designed to reduce the overhead and operating costs of the export business programme should the level of sales revenue generation fall below a predetermined point in any one quarter. It addresses areas where cost savings may be achieved and looks closely at scheduled and 'pre-approved' expense deferment issues.

Plan A should be implemented as part of the benchmark procedures previously described, and may be used as a financial control tool to redress the balance between escalating costs and reduced sales revenues, to be used as required.

Plan A offers a disciplined and pre-agreed approach to financial control of your export budget. As Plan A takes the form of a set procedure which is automatically triggered when a predetermined set of circumstances occur, i.e. failing to meet agreed sales targets, its immediate implementation will not come as a shock or surprise to anyone.

Plan B

Plan B addresses the *in extremis* scenario – when the export programme has started to go severely out of line, and you need to salvage as much as possible, either by discontinuing your export programme altogether, or by planning a major strategic retrenchment. Plan B has two basic options, and the choice of which to use depends on the severity of the situation.

Option 1

Under Option 1, you must come to terms with the fact that the export programme has not achieved its objectives, and that now – having reached the limit of available financial support – you have no alternative but to discontinue the export programme and to revert to concentrating on home markets. This essentially is a salvage operation where you endeavour to minimize the losses incurred and to recover whatever assets you can, such as stock, demonstration equipment etc.

At this point, we must issue a warning as regards discontinuing a programme. Before you make any public announcement of discontinuation, you must review every agreement, contract (e.g. joint venture documentation, distributor and/or agent agreements etc.). It is not as easy as you might think to discontinue an export business programme. Often the potential financial penalties may force you to reconsider.

Option 2

The second option of Plan B is to be employed when you have almost reached the limits of your financial support for the export programme but still have confidence in its long-term viability, and strongly believe, for whatever reason, that you need to commit further limited resources to retain a presence in the market.

Having allocated the remainder of the 'maximum fall-back' budget, you will need to restructure your export programme in order to reduce overheads to an absolute minimum and retain market presence. One way to do this is to discontinue any direct sales or marketing and restrict the programme to agent or distributor sales and/or a low-cost 'remote' third party distribution structure.

The above recommendations may appear to be rather negative, but we make no apologies for being quite blunt about the need for contingency planning. With a professionally prepared programme you should never need to resort to such drastic measures. If, however, you are forced to adopt contingency measures, a well-structured, predetermined plan will save you money and time and will be recognized as a professional approach to a very difficult problem.

THE EXPORT FINANCIAL PLAN

As we did when preparing the first draft of the export business programme, we now expand upon the topics already raised in this chapter, and address many of the additional and subsidiary issues involved in drafting and producing a 'world-class' financial plan for exporting.

The major constituents of the financial business plan are as follows.

Financial business plan

1 Introduction to financial aspects of exporting.
2 Financial objectives and time scales.
3 The initial export 'venture' costs – description and recovery procedures.
4 The fall-back figure calculations – impact on core business evaluation.
5 Detailed export budgets.
6 Cost centre allocations.
7 Projected sales revenues compared with budgets – Year 1 to Year 3.
8 a 'Hard' cash flow projection for Year 1.
  b 'Soft' cash flow projections for Years 2 and 3.

9 a 'Hard' draft P & L for Year 1.

   b 'Soft' P & L drafts for Years 2 and 3.

10 Management reporting documentation and time scales.

11 Contingency plans.

12 Conclusion.

This 12-point plan, although a little unorthodox in its content, covers almost all of the financial considerations required to effectively monitor and control finances within an overseas environment.

We now outline each section of this plan and provide additional background information and the means to implement it.

Introduction to the financial plan for export

The suggested contents of this section are as follows.

1 Introduction to topic – the need for strong financial support for the export business plan.
2 Range and scope of financial planning, controls and reporting structures.
3 How this financial plan is structured.

Financial objectives and time scales

The outline contents of this section are as follows.

1 Reaffirm and reiterate the agreed objectives list from the strategic business plan.
2 State overall financial objectives and expectations.
3 Determine your benchmark or evaluation objectives for each stage of the programme.
4 Produce a time scale for reporting, evaluation and financial reviews.

Initial 'venture' costs

The contents of this section are as follows.

1 Explain venture costs, and why they should be considered as a separate issue from the first year formal account procedures.
2 Detail what financial items should be included in the initial venture budget.

3 Explain how, and over what period of time, the initial venture costs will be recovered.

We recommend that all 'one-off' start-up costs be incorporated in an initial venture cost centre. These costs include outside consultancy fees, legal fees, and such items as basic market research costs, translation fees etc. The sum allocated for the programme start-up must be realistic and reasonable. Furthermore, the fact that this funding is allocated 'up-front' and is 'signed off' at main board director level, indicates and confirms the strong commitment from the executive management team to the export initiative.

Fall-back calculations

This section should cover the following points.

1 An explanation of the reasons for fall-back calculations – the necessity for a prudent approach.
2 How the fall-back calculations have been arrived at.

Note that in order to calculate the fall-back position you will need to review the sales projections against anticipated costs and determine a percentage figure at which you would wish to invoke fall back. Thus, it is important for you to calculate your 'on plan' point for each quarter. It is even better if you calculate this benchmark projection on a monthly basis, especially during the first six months of market entry, which is financially the most vulnerable time in any market entry.

Detailed export budgets

This section includes the following points.

1 A detailed budget for each participating department in Year 1.
2 A detailed first year summary.
3 A draft outline summary budget projection for the following two years.

Cost centre allocation

In order to prevent later misunderstandings in this section it is essential to clarify which cost centres are to be used by each department or individual. At the very least this will prevent any 'double spending' against pre-allocated budgets.

Sales revenues

This section must provide a detailed breakdown of projected sales revenues by product, by unit, by value. This information is produced in conjunction with the sales and marketing departments and may also be used as the basis for developing sales commission or agent compensation schemes.

Cash flow projection

This item is self-explanatory. Projections for Year 1 are given in detail, while those for Years 2 and 3 are in draft format.

Draft P & L

The draft P & L should be prepared in detail for Year 1 and for Years 2 and 3 in draft format.

Documentation and time scales

This section must cover the following points.

1 A list of the required weekly, monthly and quarterly financial and budget documentation.
2 A list of who should compile the various documents required, and also who has the responsibility for verification and production of the data in hard copy or digital format.
3 When the documentation should be completed.
4 The programme and calendar of financial reviews.

Contingency plans

This section covers the following items.

1 A brief description of the need for financial contingency plans.
2 Plan A – description of contents and 'trigger' points.
3 Plan B – description of contents and *in extremis* plan.

Conclusion

The concluding section must include the following points.

1 Reaffirmation of financial commitment to the strategic business plan for export.

2 Statement of thanks to contributors to the financial plan.

3 Confirmation of continuing support for the export business programme and expectation of profitable outcome.

You may wish to add items to the above suggested contents to suit specific needs within your particular industry or product sector, or you may
wish to present the items in a different order.

The above list is provided especially for companies with little or no
experience of export markets, or which have yet to develop more formal
financial procedures. Regardless of your level of experience, the issues
covered in this chapter should assist you in the creation of a 'world-class'
export financial business plan.

A final important point concerns what is perhaps one of the weakest
areas of fiscal control in export market entry programmes: the need to
tightly control overseas accounts receivable. Delays in payment can be
caused by problems associated with language, distance and time from
export market, local payment practices etc. You should follow up and
review overseas accounts receivable every day. You must insist on very
tight control from the beginning and you should have a management
programme available to implement immediately if accounts fall seriously behind schedule.

MARKET RESEARCH AND OPPORTUNITY ANALYSIS

INTRODUCTION

This chapter re-examines in greater detail some of the product and market evaluation procedures initially reviewed in the profiling formats in Chapter 8.

We have found that many overseas market entry programmes are supported by a minimum of rather basic information relating to product evaluation, market analysis and/or competitive review. Further investigation has shown that this lack of necessary information stems from ignorance of which information should be included, and how it should be analyzed, appraised and reviewed.

To ensure that your business programme documentation is complete, we provide, in this chapter, a comprehensive overview of the constituent parts of a professional market analysis and competitive evaluation by way of a complete, fully documented example – which takes you stage-by-stage through a total product evaluation process, competitive analysis and market review.

Many people contemplating export market entry believe that all they need to do, to launch their product, is to take a general overview of the potential market, and to have some outline information on competition. Nothing is further from the truth. The example documented in this chapter covers such topics as:

1 General overview of product.
2 Qualification of product to the market.
3 Product positioning – general overview.
4 Product positioning – individual countries and/or target markets.
5 Technical review.
6 Technical report on product suitability.
7 Product application review.
8 Price performance evaluation.
9 Launch pricing estimation.
10 Discount structures – general review.
11 Corporate purchase volume bulk discounts.
12 Educational and other special discounts.
13 General review of all known competition.
14 Individual competitor reviews.

15 Competitive analysis – summary.

16 Presentation of product to the market – general review.

17 Launch profile – concept presentation.

18 Potential market review.

19 Product enhancement recommendations.

20 Potential sales volume analysis.

21 Product support requirements.

22 Maintenance and repair requirements.

23 Lease and third party finance offerings.

24 Packaging and presentation.

To take just one example from the above list, product positioning and market evaluation and analysis are two areas in which, with some determined effort and application, you will gain major benefits at minimal cost. Much of the information required for market analysis is freely and readily available through the trade press, competitive brochures etc. Additional statistical information, such as important statistics, is usually available at low cost from government publications. A wide range of additional competitive information is available through competitors' advertising literature, price lists, discount structures, technical information sheets, and published specifications. All of this information may easily be gathered at competitive point-of-sale retail or wholesale locations, trade fairs, advertisements, and possibly (if applicable to your product sector) from technical reviews in a wide variety of media sources. Therefore you should ensure that you regularly see all the major publications which are dedicated to your market sector, industry or service.

The product and market evaluation takes the form of a Report, for ease of interpretation. This format also provides you with a typical example of a professional approach to this subject. If you are in any doubt as to your ability to address this area of export market entry evaluation professionally, simply follow the format of the example: include all your back-up information, analyze your information as shown in the example, and you should end up with a reasonably good result.

Pay particular attention to the competitive analysis. This is not a difficult subject and may be addressed in the following manner. Make a list of every single product feature, benefit, sales point and price information statistic for all competitors. List these in a vertical and horizontal 'comparison' chart with the names of the various competitors down the left hand side and the feature, benefit, sales points, etc. in columns across the top. (Do not forget to include your own product in this chart.) Review each competitor's information individually, then fill in the appropriate boxes for all elements of each competitor's offerings. This chart provides a very useful basic competitive analysis which you will be able to use very effectively in sales training sessions with agents, distributors and sales staff. It will also help you to identify and confirm the various sales benefits and advantages of your own products, and determine their weak points against competitive offerings. If you wish to be very professional in presenting this chart, always endeavour to present your product as the preferred best buy.

INTRODUCTION TO THE MARKET AND PRODUCT RESEARCH EXAMPLE

The example provides a detailed evaluation of part of the high-tech market sector dedicated to small portable hand-held computers. (The names of all the products and companies have been changed, and all of the data have been totally restructured in order to maintain the anonymity of the various information sources. The resulting technical details may not be totally factually correct, but this does not detract from the validity of the example. Any direct resemblance to any company, its products, specifications or services is totally unintentional.)

Our export business plan research example concerns a company which wished to enter European markets with a new offering within the palmtop computer product sector. We have renamed the product, the 'Pro-Portfolio' palm-top computer. As most readers will appreciate, the palm-top computer fills a need between desk and portable computers. It is not a personal organizer, but a compact and lightweight professional computing device in its own right. For the purpose of this exercise we have renamed the competition as follows: Reeves PS/1000, Zionics 1000, Mahusi Pocket PC, Romana Fragrana 2000, Revox Systems PCX100, Challenger 5000, Rialto ZXB, Tiatsu DD, Zarbin 5, Kohi 900 and RTS X80.

Let us first take a brief look at some extracts from the Pro-Portfolio product and competitive review which was produced in support of this market entry programme.

THE PRO-PORTFOLIO PRODUCT AND COMPETITIVE REVIEW

■ Product and competitive review

Review of palm-top computer product and market sector

Extract from product evaluation report (product definition)

In the context of this report the definition of a palm-top computer is a computing device which is capable of:

a   transfer of data;

b   offering a program language – either resident or as an optional extra.

Extract from market report

ORGANIZERS VS PALM-TOP COMPUTERS
(Product position in market sector)

The major problem in this market sector is the perceived similarity of the organizer and the computer. Possibly the simplest 'organizer' is the Rialto Computers Inc. unit. The Tiatsu Digital Diary (DD) appears to be, on technical evaluation, the most sophisticated.

Extract from competitive report

COMPETITIVE OFFERINGS
(Analysis of individual competitors)

The Zarbin Series 5 offers and actually achieves 'real computer' status by virtue of its very powerful program language (ZPL) together with a multitude of data transfer methods, between itself and another computer.

Kohi Inc. and Real-Time Systems (RTS) seem content with their version of PC compatibility, despite the very limited amount of memory available as MS-DOS system memory. On the Kohi 900 it is difficult to find more than 128K for a DOS application. On the RTS X8C, DOS programs have a little more space, but by today's standards even 256K RAM is marginal.

Extract from technical report

WINDOWS ENVIRONMENTS
(Technical evaluation – review)

Many current PC users have matured in a Windows environment. To date palm-top devices are not capable of operating Windows-based applications. This fact should be borne in mind when considering the overall market acceptability of the product. Without doubt the Pro-Portfolio falls into the 'real computer' category but the preceding comments regarding PC compatibility must be brought into the context of the required marketing strategy for this product.

The product availability within this sector for new generation palm-tops is growing at what, at first sight, seems to be an even faster rate than that for PCs. However, care must be taken to exclude the 'new case, old product' approach, as on close inspection some of the 'new range' products consist of hardware that has been available for some considerable time and has merely been repackaged – offering no more than an earlier generation product presented in new 'trendy' packaging.

One of the most significant drawbacks of portable computer equipment is battery consumption. If you have a sales force of 20, each using a device with a 10-hour battery life, they can use the device for only two hours, per day per week. Given the average cost of AA batteries as $2 then the annual cost is $100 per year per person or $2 000 for a team of 20 users.

If, however, battery life could be extended to 100 hours then the operational costs would fall to $200 per annum. It is this sort of approach that can make all the difference to the market penetration achieved.

Extract from product application report

PRODUCT APPLICATIONS

The European market is without doubt hungry for new product in this sector. It should be noted that in most cases the requirement for palm-top computers will be application driven; that is, they will be for use by field sales or service personnel. There will not be the general market as exists for the current 'portable' PC.

The cost/performance ratio must be put into the context of corporate usage for palm-tops, with the requirement of compatibility with head office PCs for those users in the field.

The above extracts indicate that the initial reports contain market information revealing the desirability of some product changes in order to promote sales and to displace competitive offerings.

The above extracts, which include several market research and product evaluation documents, were further consolidated into a product review report, given below. Before you start to compile your own market research and competitive product evaluation, take careful note of the amount of detail in the above extracts and compare it with your own findings.

The fact that the product and market sector in the example differs from your own industry sector is not relevant. It is the principle of detailed research and market evaluation that we wish to emphasize.

If the amount of detail in your own product evaluation, competitive and market research is similar to that in the example, you are clearly working from qualified information within your export business plan, and thus you should be in a position to produce an informed and well-balanced product and market review document. Our own research indicates that the reports of some exporters, even those with considerable experience, do not provide sufficient detail. We therefore expand upon the above review to provide a fully structured report, which you should be able to adapt to your own situation, whatever stage of the export market entry programme you have reached, and whatever market sector you operate in.

THE PRO-PORTFOLIO EXPORT MARKET PRODUCT EVALUATION AND MARKET REVIEW

■ Product evaluation and market review

Contents

1 Product review

2 Competitive briefing

3 Pricing

4 Product positioning

5 Potential market review

6 Product recommendations

7 Product performance expectations

8 Technical support requirements

1 Introduction and product review

There is every indication that the current market trend towards hand-held rather than lap-top computers will continue for the next two or three years in Europe. Indications are that both of the industry giants – Urivix and Xonics – are having a very close look at this market, and we anticipate that an announcement could be made by Urivix in the near future regarding a product offering.

As the Pro-Portfolio is a DOS-compatible unit we believe that any DOS-based entry by one of the major manufacturers will only add strength to this product, as it is almost certain that all the major players will go down this route in the future, rather than endeavour to superimpose new operating systems on to an already technically confused market.

Red alert

We have identified a major *red alert*. Strictly confidential enquiries to our high-tech marketing consultants, both in Europe and in the Far East, have resulted in the following information.

There are four major international companies at present which are investing heavily in CD-ROM technology. One of our best sources of information has confirmed that a hand-held (palm-top?) CD-ROM-based computer is currently being developed and is close to design/prototype completion in the Far East. This type of product has been envisaged for some time, and if it is brought to the market quickly, with a reasonable pricing, it could totally destroy the current market sector targeted for your proposed product within a period of one year from product launch.

The CD-ROM approach is regarded as the 'ultimate product' for hand-held computers, provided that a multitude of technical problems associated with this technology are overcome within a lightweight portable unit.

In our opinion, it will be some time before a true CD-ROM-based, battery-operated palm-top computer product is developed. We believe that the current information, although accurate, is more closely associated with lap-top computer development, and the work that is currently being carried out with CD-ROM 'portable books'.

The technical analysis of features and functions of the Pro-Portfolio hand-held computer product indicated to us that it is very similar to some of the current European offerings within this product sector. However, we believe that you will be able to develop some unique, and 'added value' sales points provided that special attention is paid to the following items.

1 Re-engineered case design.

2 Capability of information exchange to PCs.

Most of the current 11 European offerings in the palm-top computer sector are aimed mainly at child and student markets. These 11 offerings are divided approximately 60–40 into personal organizers and palm-top computers.

2 Competitive briefing

There is a great deal of confusion at present in this area of the market as to what is a true palm-top computer and what is an organizer. Competition has exacerbated this situation, resulting in the designing of products which seem to offer optimum solutions in both areas. However, most of these multi-functional products are neither very good personal organizers nor good quality palm-top computers.

Furthermore, the wide variety of buttons and keys needed to access the multitude of non-related functions in organizer and computer combinations causes even more confusion. As the Pro-Portfolio is essentially a palm-top computer, we see this product as being in direct competition only with similar computer type products. However, some manufacturers of dual-purpose products portray them as offering the best of both worlds. This is very confusing to the consumer.

Summary of competitive analysis

In summary, the current offerings in this market appear to leave substantial room for a new more technically advanced product such as the Pro-Portfolio which could have vast appeal to the majority of potential purchasers due to its DOS-based system 3.5" floppy drive and direct compatibility and interface capability with desktop units.

We believe that you should make every endeavour to position the Pro-Portfolio product as the only real offering in the marketplace that enables a user to have full control and command of his computer facilities from a palm-top computer – right through to distributed PC networks (LANs and WANs).

In addition you should also emphasize the competition's lack of ability to communicate via modems and thus endeavour to establish this product as the lead product for Europe for all sales and technical people who spend the majority of their time in the field. This is the major market for multiple high-volume sales in Europe.

Research

In order to prepare this competitive briefing, we researched all known and current offerings within the portable computer market, both in the UK and throughout Europe. These totalled some 20 products in all. The secondary evaluation, which focused more closely on 'professional' hand-held computer devices, reduced this figure to 11, after we had discarded the low end market offerings which were targeted at children and very young students. The 11 offerings are divided approximately 60–40 into personal organizers and palm-top computers.

Competitive listing

We further refined the 11 products down to six and focused on what we believe to be your main competition within the true palm-top computer area. These are as follows: Reeves PS/1000, Zionics 1000, Mahusi Pocket PC, Romana Fragrana 2000, Revox Systems PCX100 and Challenger 5000.

Competition – European distribution

The six main competitive units are currently available in Europe. It is very difficult (almost impossible) to determine true distribution statistics as, once a product has been cleared into a Common Market member country, it is then free to circulate throughout all EC member countries.

However, as all six units are qualified as available in the UK, we assume that distribution throughout Europe is already in place through named distributors and agents. This is obviously the case with the major manufacturers such as Zionics and Challenger, which already have comprehensive European coverage via their own dealer network and retailing chains.

Prime competitor

We see the Zionics 1000 as your main competitor as it is the only palm-top computer which currently has a hard disk and one of the very few with the capability to input/output to a 3.5" floppy drive. In addition, it is also one of the very few palm-top computers similar to your product which incorporates a screen capable of displaying an entire DOS screen set.

A major detraction from the Zionics palm-top offering is the addition of sockets for a microphone and headset which provide a built-in recording system. We see this as very much a gimmick – as this feature using the hard disk to store spoken commands does not appear to be very easy to use, reliable in use or at all relevant for most business applications.

Analysis of prime competitor's product

Having identified the Zionics 1000 as your major competitor in terms of features and functions, we further analyzed this product against the Pro-Portfolio to establish key sales 'knock-off' points. These are as follows.

- Size: The Zionics 1000 s rather too big to be a palm-top computer. In fact it is very s milar in size to some of the current fully configured lap-top computers.

- Case: The case of the Zionics 1000 is poorly engineered and not very durable or strong for a 'portable' device.

- Weight: At 1275g we consider the Zionics 1000 too heavy to be called a palm-top computer.

- Battery life: The quoted battery life is only 1.5 to 3.6 hours. (We cannot understand this large variance – is it application or power sensitive? Perhaps your technical staff could advise upon this.) This feature alone prevents the Zionics 1000 from being a true lightweight portable palm-top computer which you can use anywhere, unless you want to carry several pocketfuls of batteries with you!

A final point regarding the Zion cs offering is that no new software has been developed for the 1000 product. Yet again the US giant announced a 'new' product but it uses refurbished software previously developed for Zionics lap-top computers – which were originally launched in Europe almost seven years ago.

This comment is not a direct competitive sales 'knock-off- point, but you should be aware that the current rumblings in the Zionics financial empire suggest that they are highly sensitive to cash flow. Thus, wherever you encounter the Zionics 1000 in direct competition to the Pro-Portfolio, you will find that Zionics will consider and offer quite astounding discounts to win a deal. Please note that your current market entry finance plan already provides for a maximum 30 per cent discount. If you exceed this discount level in direct head-to-head competition with Zionics in single unit sales, you will not cover your sales costs and operating overheads for market entry to Europe.

We suggest that you counter this direct assault from multi-layer discounting by providing the purchaser with a free diskette-based 'user friendly' software training package. This should not only cover all aspects of the Pro-Portfolio's operation, but also include information and instructions on all of your additional plug-in products, providing you with a superb opportunity to present the selling points of all your products and added-value items.

3 Pricing

Your current launch price is scheduled to be US$1150. This places you in almost the most expensive position for this type of product in Europe. (The current Zionics product is priced at $1250, but this recommended retail price is normally pre-sale discounted to below $1100.) So the Pro-Portfolio, at a price of $1150, will be the most expensive in Europe. This top price could be a sales benefit if the product is packaged and presented correctly, together with the added value offerings and additional plug-in devices.

Launch price revision

However, regardless of the above comment, we recommend that it would be safer to review and reduce your launch pricing by 5 per cent to bring your product into the European market at just under the current Zionics discounted 'first offer' retail price.

Discount structure

We note from your discount structure that you have made provision for up to 30 per cent on a direct discount scale. We recommend you to hold at least 50 per cent of this in hand at present, and to reappraise the situation six months after launch. This will have two consequences. It will prevent the competition from knowing your overall pricing and discount strategy policy. It will also give you the flexibility of reducing the price by a large amount at one time. Such a strategy tends to unnerve the competition, they do not know how many times you are going to do this before you put them out of business!

Multiple sales (bulk sales) discount structure

Our specific recommendation regarding bulk sales to multinational or similar large (major account) organizations in Europe is that you announce a very attractive pricing package for such organizations. As you will appreciate, we have already defined this sales sector as being the most significant opportunity for major sales achievements.

We believe that your current pricing strategy and discount structure are inappropriate. We recommend that you immediately offer a corporate discount with a scale based on a minimum 10 units plus for 'one-off' bulk contract sales, with further discount breaks at 20, 50, 100, 200, 500 and 1000 units. We recommend that this 'major account' pricing package be incorporated within a 'special applications' based brochure developed by your marketing department to maximize on all the feature and function benefits of the product and the price performance gains in productivity for users in large organizations.

In real terms you could almost forget about developing a third party distribution network for this product in Europe (with all its associated problems), if you focus on and confirm your market with many of the large European corporate companies. This will automatically (through the wide geographic distribution of such organizations throughout Europe) greatly enhance your overall European market penetration, and give you further European sales coverage. (Please note however that, if you focus on major account sales you must be able to support the product both technically, and with maintenance support throughout Europe.)

We further recommend the close involvement of your technical department in preparing this special corporate sales offering – to maximize on the benefits of a DOS-based system, plus plug-in 3.5" hard disk unit and the enormous benefits to be gained through a high-speed plug-in comms-link modem. Although these features have very little to do with pricing we feel the outcome of this major account opportunity will be crucial to your market establishment in Europe and you should make the most of this opportunity.

Educational discounts

Some final comments on pricing. There is quite a growth market in Europe within schools, universities, education colleges etc. We recommend that, using the 'cradle to grave' principles first established by such companies as IBM, in their special educational discount programmes, you look very closely at preparing a special pricing structure solely for educational establishments. You could offer a further option, that a student or child could purchase his or her palm-top computer direct from their school at the special educational discounted price. Although this practice will be abused, it will allow you to capture still further market share which would almost certainly have gone directly to your main competitors.

We believe that there is merit in this approach. It will enable you not only to develop substantial educational sales, but also to automatically increase your market share through parents of children or students purchasing your product on their behalf. An example of how successful such education programmes can be is fully documented in the Zionics 'Educational Establishment' literature. Similar examples may be obtained from IBM and the BBC range of computers in the UK.

We suggest that for these bulk purchases you trim your profits heavily and aim for a maximum 10 per cent net per unit. Such pricing would strike very hard at all known competition in Europe and truly establish your product as the lead palm-top computer in all major European countries.

4 Product positioning

We believe that you will appreciate that, as this is your only major product in this market sector, it would be extremely difficult, and from a credibility viewpoint inappropriate, to present this product as part of a fully integrated product set – overlaid with 'future' new offerings. This may not be to your disadvantage, as you will be able to position the Pro-Portfolio as a product which is capable of integrating into any DOS-based PC environment. In general terms we would position the Pro-Portfolio product at the mid-to-top range of offerings both on price and quality. We believe you will agree that it seems appropriate to position the product as follows:

> The Pro-Portfolio is not single manufacturer operating system dependent. Thus we have been able to select all the best features and functions currently used in professional PC environments and incorporate them in this new and unique product. Due to the product design we are also able to utilize almost all standard software that has been developed in DOS. Thus, the user has total flexibility in choice of software and is not restricted to any one manufacturer's software platform. In addition the buyer may select from a comprehensive range of Pro-Portfolio approved and certified plug-in modules: modems, printers, fax boards and CD-ROM. Again, as all Pro-Portfolio interfaces are industry standard, purchasers are not limited to one manufacturer for additional functions or I/O devices.

Note that if you adopt this marketing platform, you must ensure that a non-liability clause is inserted in all your sales orders and contracts regarding use of 'Non Pro-Portfolio' add-ons.

You should give major emphasis to the wide range of 'plug-in' and 'add-on' options which you have developed for your product, as these offer potential users a unique development capability and route for functional enhancement.

The 'ultimate solution' approach

An advertising approach to the European markets presenting your product as 'The ultimate solution in palm-top computers' would maximize on all your product features and plug-in enhancements. This should quickly establish your product as the preferred technical response. (Please note, however, that whenever your sales or marketing staff provide this product to the media for technical review it is essential to include the full range of accessories, plug-in modules and additional software enhancements – as these are one of your major marketing sales strengths. If these are not supplied, we believe you will enjoy only a mediocre or lukewarm response from reviewers.)

5 Potential market review

The geographic distribution analysis of the total current market in Europe for palm-top and organizer computer products is set out in Table 12.1.

Table 12.1 Market for palm-top computers and organizers in Europe

Country	All hand products (%)	Palm-top products(%)
United Kingdom	17	5
France	21	6
Germany	20	6
Spain	9	3
The Netherlands	16	5
Italy	4	1
Scandinavia	6	2
Rest of Europe	7	2
Total	100	30

6 Product recommendations

We believe that your current overall design criteria for the Pro-Portfolio is excellent, in that you have not tried to overlay a pocket organizer on to a hand-held computer.

Future development should concentrate on all the ways in which it would be possible to re-configure or enhance your product so that it has the true facility of rapid information exchange between the Pro-Portfolio and a customer's desktop computer, file server or in-house LAN. Almost all of our market researchers highlighted this point as a central, and very major issue with almost all corporate potential purchasers.

Training enhancement recommendation

As the product has the capability of a 'plug-in' 3.5" floppy drive, why do you not consider putting a full user training course, to cover every feature and machine function in detail, on a 3.5" disk, and give it free with each unit? This, together with some new visuals to upgrade the handbook, would give you a 'first' in this market sector – as no other manufacturer appears to have done this.

7 Product performance expectations

Volume analysis

Volume analysis is extremely difficult because not only are there multiple entry points into Europe for products such as yours but some manufacturers have already established manufacturing and assembly operations within Europe.

Thus, it is virtually impossible to determine market shares and volumes from import statistics. However, we have arrived at the following conclusions.

EC volume assumptions

We have to make some volume assumptions for this product group in Europe. (Please see our previous comments on EC distribution.) Historically companies such as Zionics, Challenger and Kohi have only brought new products to the market when they have been confident of potential minimum sales throughout Europe of over 2000 units per month.

The major European market for this specialist hand-held computer product group is shared between Zionics, Challenger and Kohi. The current ratios of distribution appear to be fairly equal, and we project that individually they have between 20 per cent and 25 per cent of the current market. In addition, there are a few outsiders, Tiatsu and Revox being the foremost amongst these. Due to Tiatsu's more extensive distribution network we anticipate that the remaining 25 per cent is shared in a ratio of 65–35 in favour of Tiatsu.

8 Technical support requirements

As stated previously in relation to pricing, if you wish to maximize on sales opportunities for this product in Europe it is essential that you address the 'major account' opportunities. Such a strategy has special implications for technical support and service requirements.

As most of the top 1000 companies in Europe have operations in many countries, you must have the capability to service this product wherever it is used – regardless of where it was sold. For example, you may have closed a bulk discount order with Drenig Household Appliance GmbH (DHA) in Germany for use by their appointed maintenance and service outlets to record spares and replacement requirements. You are aware that DHA distribute their products throughout mainland Europe, but you may not realize that DHA product distribution also includes Greece, Portugal, Eire, the Balearic Islands, Iceland and Eastern Europe, so you need to address the issues of technical and maintenance support on a much wider basis than you at first envisaged, in your draft export business plan.

Maintenance and service support

The mechanics of establishing maintenance and service support may be accomplished by appointing service agents in all appropriate countries. However your real problem is in the area of direct 'user' support. To underpin your service agent network you may wish to consider utilizing the services of one of the major

European logistics companies to put together a 'total solution' transportation offering for service and/or repair.

User support

We recommend that you consider setting up a 'European hot line' call centre facility which covers all mainland (and outer) Europe based on local 'in-country' telephone dial-ups. In order to keep costs to a minimum we further recommend that this user facility be offered on a telephone line call charge facility similar to that operated by many information providers and technical support groups throughout Europe, whereby the first ten minutes are free, the remainder chargeable. We also recommend that, in addition to establishing the 'hot line' call centre facility, you provide specialist support on site for all major accounts. If this support was structured to provide 'key trainer' training for some of the technical staff of your major accounts, you would greatly reduce your cost overheads.

....

The main message of the above sample report is that, as with a computer, you only achieve good output from good input. The better the quality of and the more detailed your research, the more likely it is that you will produce a high quality and professional business plan.

In concluding this chapter we provide a checklist which should cover almost all product types and market sectors. If you operate in a highly specialized area, you may need to add to the list to cover any special product or market requirements.

Product and market analysis

1 **General overview of product** ☐

2 **Qualification of product to the market** ☐

3 **Product positioning – general overview** ☐

4 **Product positioning – individual countries and target markets** ☐

5 **Technical review** ☐

6 **Technical report on product suitability** ☐

7 **Product application review** ☐

8 **Price performance evaluation** ☐

9 **Launch pricing estimation** ☐

10	Discount structures – general review	☐
11	Corporate purchase volume bulk discounts	☐
12	Educational and special discounts	☐
13	General review of all known competition	☐
14	Individual competitor reviews	☐
15	Competitive analysis – summary	☐
16	Presentation of product to the market – general review	☐
17	Launch profile – concept presentation	☐
18	Potential market review	☐
19	Product enhancement recommendations	☐
20	Potential sales volume analysis	☐
21	Product support requirements	☐
22	Maintenance and repair requirements	☐
23	Lease and third party finance offerings	☐
24	Packaging and presentation review	☐
25	Translation requirements	☐
26	Cultural and religious sensitivity check	☐
27	Special import regulations check (technology restrictions?)	☐
28	Order all market sector publications	☐
29	Daily media check for anything in your market sector	☐
30	Spares, returns, maintenance logistics	☐
31	Training requirements check	☐

This lengthy checklist reflects the very wide variety of issues and subsidiary topics which need to be covered in relation to product and market analysis.

Once again, we stress the need to achieve sales in your intended export market. Good market analysis and attention to your product positioning will give you the very best possible start with your sales programme. Do not underestimate the power of the Need, Feature, Benefit analysis, in the form of a quick ready-reference grid. You must provide your sales staff, your agents and distributors with ammunition for fighting the competition, but before you print anything concerning your competition, make sure it is all marked 'Company Confidential'. If you do not want to face legal actions, thoroughly check your competitive 'knock-off' points before inclusion in any documentation intended for third party, public or general distribution.

REVIEW OF PLANNING AND PREPARATION FOR SALES AND MARKETING

INTRODUCTORY REVIEW

This chapter takes the form of a programme mid-point review. This review is very necessary, both to reconfirm and to reinforce the important strategic issues relating to export market entry, and to provide a formal introduction to the remaining chapters which concentrate almost exclusively upon the wide variety of methods of achieving sales and distribution of your products, goods and services in your new overseas market.

Throughout the previous chapters we have focused mainly on the preparation of an export business plan and an export financial plan. You should now understand the major requirements for preparing a professional export business plan and recognize the need to support that business plan with a well structured financial business plan.

To effect a professional and cost-effective entry into a new overseas market may not be quite as simple as you first envisaged: many product and market factors need to be carefully considered, together with other issues such as market size, lead product qualification and pricing.

However, we believe that by closely following the plans, programmes and procedures outlined, you will be able to avoid almost all of the major pitfalls, and through detailed and comprehensive documentation in the form of the third draft of your strategic export business plan (and its accompanying financial business plan), you will now be in a position to create your own 'route map' – individually tailored to your own company's products and market sector – for export market entry.

We provide below a brief summary and review of Part 2, in the form of a checklist. Please review this carefully before proceeding, as the omissions from your strategic business plan for export, of matters considered in previous chapters, will prevent, or hinder you from implementing many of the sales and marketing programmes addressed in the following chapters.

Review of business and financial plans

1 **Export plan definition**   ☐

2 **Objective setting**   ☐

3 **The qualification of export objectives**   ☐

4 **Positioning your market entry**   ☐

5   Qualifying your export capabilities ☐

6   Standard inclusions for first draft of business plan ☐

7   Additional information requirements ☐

8   Profiling formats ☐

9   Product and market analysis formats ☐

10 Second draft of strategic business plan ☐

11 Business mission statement ☐

12 Financial mission statement ☐

13 Qualification of export market potentials ☐

14 Market evaluation and analysis – options ☐

15 Relationships with information providers ☐

16 Market potential evaluation ☐

17 Potential market sizing ☐

18 Geographical analysis ☐

19 Determining market maturity ☐

20 Introduction to competitive activity ☐

21 Market expansion potential ☐

22 Cultural and religious factors ☐

23 Economic sensitivity ☐

24 Measurement of product potential ☐

25 Lead product evaluation ☐

26 Financial procedures ☐

27 Financial considerations for exporters ☐

28 Strategic financial planning ☐

29 Minimizing the risk factors ☐

30 Financial objectives ☐

31 Export budgets and costs ☐

32 Financial measurement and control routines ☐

33 Financial contingency planning ☐

34 Evaluation of potential financial exposures ☐

35 Determination of financial benchmarks ☐

36 Calculation of financial fall-back position ☐

37 Constituents of the export finance plan ☐

38 Export market – accounts receivable ☐

39 Market research and opportunity analysis ☐

40 Final draft of strategic business plan ☐

41 In-depth market analysis ☐

The topic of market and product evaluation and positioning is quite difficult to present in a user friendly and readily acceptable format, especially if this is your first venture into exporting. However, we believe that Chapter 12 provides a good example of a professional and very comprehensive evaluation report. The Pro-Portfolio example should enable you to prepare a high quality, accurate and well presented market and product evaluation report.

Pay particular attention to developing the drafts of your strategic business plan, and always attempt to qualify all items as closely as possible to your own products and individual business sector.

The finance plan is self-explanatory. You must be rigorous in qualifying export budgets and costs against expected sales revenues. It pays to be ruthless in assessing anticipated revenues against costs, but – regardless of the methodology you use – always try to remain practical and objective. Strive at all times to recognize sales and marketing issues: after all, you are on the same side. A first-class overseas financial business plan will do more than anything else to help you achieve success. Always remember: exporting is about profit realization.

PREPARATION FOR SALES AND MARKETING

The final part of this book provides very detailed treatment of sales and marketing issues, covering almost everything which you will require in order to sell your products effectively in your chosen export market.

The success of your export business programme is dependent, in the main, upon just three factors:

- A professional market entry programme.
- A comprehensive financial plan.
- The ability to implement the programme in the chosen market and secure sales.

By now you should realize that we believe that the achievement of a good sales result is the key to consolidation of new export markets. You may spend much time and money in developing all of the necessary documentation, procedures, and business plans, but all the planning, preparation and personal commitment will be to no avail if you fail to sell your products in your chosen market. In the following chapters we examine many of the factors which could possibly affect your sales results.

Selling in any market is all about sales activity – not only the sales programmes and the activities which promote the sales of products, but also the sales support routines that must be in place to effectively support the purchaser after the product has been sold. Any problems associated with sales or sales support that you experience in your home market, will be magnified in an export market. In distant markets, there are no 'quick fix' solutions, no fast customer follow-up procedures, and no dynamic and direct account management and control procedures, such as you have in home markets. If you fail to support customers effectively in your export markets you will quickly lose your initial market share, and you will rapidly head towards market exit. Failure to provide effective customer support and service will create additional problems. You could end up with a number of very dissatisfied customers who not only require, but legally demand a level of product support and assistance which is both very time consuming and very expensive.

The above comments are of particular relevance to anyone involved in any way with 'technical' or system-based products. In this area of export sales, closing the sale is only the first step: professional account consolidation is vital if you are to expand your market and a customer recommendation should be highly prized. Dedication and persistence in the pursuit of customer satisfaction must be at the forefront of an exporter's mind at all times.

183

Part 3

SALES AND MARKETING PROGRAMMES

ACHIEVING SALES IN
EXPORT MARKETS

This chapter reviews the selection of overseas sales staff and some general overseas sales and marketing plans.

SELECTION OF OVERSEAS SALES STAFF

The initial selection of staff for your export sales programme is of great importance as the quality and level of experience of the staff will have a significant effect upon the outcome of your programme. The member of staff who pioneers the export programme overseas is a key appointee and must, of course, be sufficiently mature to deal with all aspects of the appointment.

If your product is of a technical nature always try to select someone with proven technical knowledge. There is nothing more embarrassing than to face a potential sales prospect who appears to know far more about the technology in which you are involved than you do. The person selected must ensure that they have full knowledge of all relevant technical and pricing information. (The same applies to you, if yours is a one-person operation.) If you cannot find the right mixture of sales and technical skills in one person, it is far safer to appoint two people with complementary skills.

Many sales and technical staff rightly perceive involvement in exporting as a promotion. The position demands respect, for developing a business overseas takes a great deal more resilience and courage than operating in home markets, is fraught with many potential problems and most certainly requires much harder work. If a staff member has reservations about working overseas, however, never put pressure on them to do so.

If a staff member selected for an overseas appointment is married, it is wise to discuss the overseas opportunity with both partners at an early stage. Not all relationships can survive prolonged periods of separation. The same is true of your own close relationships if yours is a one-person operation.

Pay your export staff well and allow reasonable expenses. Work hard and play hard is a good maxim, but a balance must be achieved so that job performance and the business mission are not affected.

PLANNING THE FIRST OVERSEAS SALES VISIT

Take time to put together a good itinerary. Make sure that all appointments – both sales and commercial – are confirmed by both fax and telephone or telex, prior to departure from your home country, and that an individual briefing and information and brochure pack is prepared for each appointment.

There is a physical limit to the amount of literature and/or information packs you can take with you so you should be discriminating when handing out information packs. If you plan a market 'blitz', send the information packs by separate carrier to your hotel well beforehand, and confirm their arrival by fax or telex prior to departure.

Your first visit after arrival should be to your embassy commercial department. This will not only effect a commercial introduction but provide you with access to help in the event of personal crisis, difficulty or hardship.

Do not overcrowd your programme. If you have too many appointments you will not have time to complete your programme to a high standard of professionalism. You should always allow for delays and programme changes and you should allow yourself some time to recover from jet lag and to relax. There should also be sufficient time for you to review your strategy before calls and to assess progress afterwards. You should try to limit the number of calls to two or at a maximum three per day.

You should not expect, on your first visit to your new market, to make many sales. The prime objective is to obtain one confirmed order. This first order will enable you to initiate, test and confirm all of your export order processing routines and logistics – in order to thoroughly validate all the arrangements for order processing and programme support at your home country head office. You need an *order* to be able to do this; a 'trial', or requests for samples, are not sufficient.

Another very valuable aspect of a sales order, right at the start of your programme, is that it adds credibility to your sales presentations, and proves to potential customers that you are serious about developing your export business.

To achieve your first order you may have to sell at a reduced (discounted) price, but remember, this is a pre-agreed strategic sales decision.

Your preliminary research should have enabled you to identify the major purchasers in your chosen market. You should plan to secure the order from one of these major companies if possible. A sale to a major company is far better than a sale to a minor organization or an unknown company. If you are forced to achieve this first order on a reduced margin, you should aim for the best possible sales reference right from the outset. If you are successful with this strategy, it will stand you in very good stead when you come to expand your foothold in your new market.

Having secured this first important order you now have to make it work for you. To do this, you must develop this opportunity into a totally satisfied customer. Check carefully that all the order processes work and ensure that everyone understands that closing the order is just the start. The process that follows is called order reinforcement. As soon as the order is secured, you must ensure that the customer knows that this is an important first order for you, and that you want to work closely with them to ensure an excellent result for all concerned. Exhibit your professionalism – not only through first-class sales presentations and negotiating skills, but also by your 'confirmed' personal involvement and commitment.

Having completed the normal sales and purchasing negotiations, you should ask to be introduced to the customer's financial controller and/or financial director (build a relationship here and you will always be paid). Also seek an introduction to the customer's technical manager or director and take every opportunity to ensure that your own technical staff meet with the customer's technical staff. If both companies' technical staff get on well together (and that often means through mutual technical respect) you will have the very best of 'salespeople' working internally as a team for you.

We now provide a travel checklist for your first overseas sales visit.

Export travel: mandatory items for first sales visit to new export market

1 Medical matters

a Have a full medical (including cardiograph) and dental check-up. ☐

b If you wear any form of reading glasses, contact lenses or dentures purchase a second pair. ☐

c If you take any form of regularly prescribed medication ensure that you have at least double the required amount for the duration of your intended stay, and divide this up between your luggage and your briefcase. Some countries' drug laws ban some standard prescription drugs without a letter of

authorization from a doctor so, if you are concerned that you
may be affected, seek advice from the country's embassy
before your departure. ☐

d Check and confirm that your overseas medical repatriation
insurance covers your intended area of travel. ☐

e If necessary take anti-malaria medication (check with your
doctor). ☐

f Complete the series of inoculations for your destination
country: do you have a current and valid international
vaccination certificate? ☐

2 Passport: check that this is valid and in date. ☐

3 Visa: check this for entry and exit dates, and ensure that it is
the correct type of visa. ☐

4 Reservations: check all reservations, including air tickets,
hotels, car hire, onward travel etc., and ensure that you take
all fax/telex confirmations with you. If you plan to drive yourself
(strongly not recommended in many countries) check whether
you need an international driving licence or a certified translation
of your home country licence or driving document. ☐

5 Credit cards: do you have sufficient limit on your cards for your
estimated expenditure plus at least 100 per cent for contingencies?
A full international VISA card is strongly recommended as many
foreign hotels and retail establishments do not accept many of
the more exclusive cards because of their high commission
charges. ☐

6 Currency: always take a small amount of local currency with you,
plus at least US$500 cash as back-up, in addition to travellers
cheques (US$ preferably). ☐

7 Sales visits: have you everything you require for these? Remember
to prepare a separate portfolio for each scheduled call. Take
plenty of letter heads, business cards, compliment slips. If you
require the use of a PC, don't forget the special multiplug
electrical connector, and if you use e-mail or a fax modem for
communications with your head office you will also need the

191

> **special multiplug adapter/converter for non-western hotel phone sockets.** ☐
>
> 8 **Ensure that you leave a list of all of your credit cards, travellers cheque numbers, passport and visa etc. in the company safe with your financial director.** ☐

The above eight-point plan must be completed by everyone who intends to travel to overseas markets. It should be regarded as the minimum pre-travel programme review.

Finally, very briefly, we would like to summarize our advice on personal conduct, based on many years' experience. This is simply to be professional – to be diplomatic in the expression of your views, to brief yourself thoroughly on the major issues under discussion in your targeted country and to take no risks with your personal safety.

EXPORT MARKET ENTRY
SALES CALLS

PRE-PLANNING

The prime objective of your first overseas visit is, of course, to obtain the first vital order. Allow sufficient time, before setting out on your first sales call, to review each of your prospect files for the day. You should at this stage try to assess which points are the 'hot buttons' you will need to address to achieve that order.

In preparation for your visit you will have acquired some background information on your targeted country. You should also learn to greet people confidently in their own language. To be able to say 'Hello, I'm very pleased to meet you' will win you respect from your prospective buyer – especially if they know this is your first visit to their country. Even very difficult languages can be broken down into phonetics, and a member of staff at your hotel will usually be very happy to help you – for free or for a small gratuity.

You should not arrange a full schedule for your first day. This will enable you to recover somewhat from your journey. You can use this day to confirm appointments, visit your country's embassy, have some exercise, light meals and an early night. If you cannot avoid a meeting, do not undertake any formal negotiations on this occasion, when you may be more tired than you realize.

It has been known for a local business contact to arrange a very busy schedule (including evening entertainment) for a visiting exporter, intentionally putting physical and psychological pressure on the seller, with the aim of achieving the best possible terms for the local party.

SALES TECHNIQUES

This is not a sales manual so we leave the structure of your sales calls to your individual style and professional technique. However, as many people have asked us for advice concerning their first sales calls, we include an overview of some proven sales techniques. (Bear in mind this chapter is addressed to those whose sales experience is relatively limited.)

The fundamental point about all successful sales negotiations is that you need to identify the prospective customer's needs, qualify these needs against the features of your product or service and convince the prospective customer of the benefits to be gained by purchasing your offering. This is called Need, Feature, Benefit (NFB) analysis. Even if you are not very experienced in selling, if you follow this basic formula you will not go too far wrong.

IDENTIFYING AND CONFIRMING NEEDS

You should try to identify a prospective customer's needs before your visit. (The only exception to this rule is the 'cold call'.) Then try to get prospects to identify their needs themselves by open questions and you will be able to qualify the need for change. Open questions seek a response, such as 'What do you think about x?', as opposed to closed questions, such as 'Have you tried an XYZ?', that elicit a 'yes' or 'no' response. You need to invite comment and discourse through open questions. If you are selling any product or service and you do not establish a need for your offering you will never close a sale.

Establishment of qualified needs is the basis for successful order closing – especially in export markets. Ignore this and your selling job becomes almost insurmountable. In broad terms, successful qualification of needs requires at least 60 per cent of the conversation to come from your prospective customer. It is vital that your prospective customer recognize for themselves the need(s) to acquire your product or service or to change from another supplier.

A professional exporter will carefully note the identified needs, particularly the 'hot buttons' when the eyes light up and the prospective customer becomes voluble in explaining problems, bad experiences or requirements. All too often, however, an exporter overlooks the customer's statement of needs in the rush to present the product or offering.

With the need identified, your next step is to qualify that need. This is not the time to expand upon the features of your product. Your approach should be subtle:

> 'If I could show you a way of overcoming – getting a better result – more performance – increased sales – better product – better quality – more reliability etc. . . . at a realistic price, would you be interested?'

If you have gone through the needs identification and qualification process in a professional manner the only logical response is 'yes'. If you do not receive this response you must return to needs to ensure that your customer recognizes the weaknesses in their present operations and, therefore, why they need your product or service.

IDENTIFYING FEATURES

Having established and qualified the need, you may then present the features of your product or service. Depending on the circumstances, you may think it best to start with minor features and build up, leaving the best until last, but in another situation it may be better to concentrate on the main feature. This is a matter for your own judgement.

In presenting features you need to have a sales kit, whatever your position in your company. For those of you who may be unfamiliar with sales kits, the following overview may be helpful. Within the framework of a loose leaf binder or presentation folder, a professional sales kit should contain pages of information, photographs, diagrams etc. which you require to visually support and reinforce your presentation. Often your approach is of the 'Story Book' type – commencing with a brief outline of your company, with photographs (full colour) of your production or office facilities, your products, systems or services and examples of customer installations. There should also be a list of satisfied customers.

In your presentation – preferably with the aid of your sales kit – always try to reinforce features by qualifying them against established needs, for example:

> 'As you can see from this [photograph, picture, diagram] we recognized this problem or need which you have already identified and have designed/modified our product so that you can . . .'

or

> 'Here is an example from one of our customers who has . . .'

Technical staff involvement in sales call or presentation

If your product is of a technical nature, a technically qualified person should present the technical features, but you should ensure your prospective customer is accompanied by technical staff.

If your technical staff take part in the sales presentation, allow them to present the technical features in their own way. Sales orientated people are often tempted to interrupt their technical staff because they see their technical presentation as not sufficiently sales oriented. This is a major mistake. The technical presentation is often accepted as valid for the very reason that the technical person is *not* a sales person. The result may well be the placement of an order.

BENEFITS AND ORDER CLOSING

It is important, in presenting the benefits of your product, to be realistic, and not to exaggerate or be repetitive. Sales have been lost in this way.

The subject of Need, Feature, Benefit analysis and the associated sales techniques could fill a book on its own, but this overview gives you a start. You also need awareness of body language, interactive psychology and human relationship issues, as well as skill in professional questioning techniques. We recommend that, regardless of your seniority, you should take a course and learn professional sales techniques.

Finally, a conscientious, hard working person (even one who makes some mistakes) will be respected for their honesty and integrity and will often gain orders because buyers feel 'safe' with them.

DEVELOPING SALES OF A LEAD PRODUCT OR SERVICE

POST-SALES VISIT REPORT

As soon as possible after your first sales call, and every subsequent call, you must review the meeting and write up your sales call notes. One major reason for limiting yourself to two or three visits per day is to allow yourself time to compile this vital post-sales visit report.

It is vital to impose this strict discipline upon yourself while the details are fresh, and not to delay. Many people (especially senior and executive staff) feel that in their position they should not need to write up sales call reports or visit notes. On the contrary, they should always prepare their own notes in a professional and comprehensive manner.

We set out below the minimum requirements of a post-sales visit report (PSVR).

It is a good idea to prepare the format of the PSVR on a PC in your own company style before your overseas visit, and run off sufficient blank copies to cover all your scheduled sales calls plus spares for additional contacts.

The PSVR contains three types of information.

1 Background information on customer.
2 Details of meeting.
3 Further action list.

Customer background

The first section of the PSVR contains background information about your customer, prospect or business contact: name and address of company visited, telephone, fax, telex numbers, contact list at meeting (names, initials, titles etc.), date and time of meeting, additional contacts made or noted etc. This 'standard' section contains all the information you will require to renew contacts at a later date. Be particularly careful with this section and try to capture as much basic information as possible – especially contact names.

Much of this information may be included in your pre-visit individual meeting pack, but it is very useful to cross-check and if necessary update your information base.

You may be tempted to use a portable computer or a personal organizer to record, organize and update all your visit, prospect and customer information files. However, it is our experience that although these are first-class business tools, they are very easily damaged or stolen. If you do use one of these units, carry it with you at all times. Do not leave it in your hotel room or use it in the hotel bar. A hard copy is much safer, and you can input the information to your computer or personal organizer later on, and still retain a back-up hard copy as security.

Portable PC disk drives 'crash' quite often, through being dropped, or otherwise roughly handled during travel. Always back up your information on to diskettes and store them separately from your computer. If you are working as part of a team, give an additional 'back-up' copy diskette to your partner to keep for you. Never use a personal organizer for important data storage that does not have a 'file transfer' capability. If the mother board goes down you have lost everything – as it is almost totally impossible to retrieve recorded information in this circumstance.

Meeting details

The second part of the PSVR contains information on what actually happened at the meeting: the items discussed, and the list of established and identified needs. It is vital to record this information. This section does not need to be long but must give all the facts. If you did not achieve your main objectives, say so and explain the reasons.

Further action list

The final part of the PSVR is the further actions list, covering everything from the despatch of a brochure to the careful follow-up of a good potential sales opportunity. You cannot be expected to remember the details of what you have promised to do. List and record intended actions.

Ensuring that all of the paperwork is completed is an important part of overseas business development and is vital for follow-up activities. As it is always possible that someone other than you will be undertaking the follow-up you should ensure that your PSVR is totally professional.

SECONDARY BUSINESS DEVELOPMENT PROGRAMME

We now turn to the rest of your planned sales programme. You must be prepared to make changes in your schedule – for all sorts of reasons, whether related to travel problems, the unexpected absence of an interpreter or other unforeseen eventualities. So long as your schedule is not too tight, however, you should be able to accommodate changes and still be able to achieve at least 70 per cent of your scheduled calls. So, having completed your PSVR, what do you do with the rest of your time? This is when you pursue your secondary or 'fall-back' programme and embark upon some 'cold calls'. This is one of the more exciting aspects of overseas business development and you never know where it will lead you until you try.

Unless you are in a position to sell off your samples by direct cold call approaches, we recommend that you take the risk of possibly receiving an order and use the phone. Very often, because you are a foreigner, people know that your time is limited and will quite often go out of their way to see you. Even if you do not close an order immediately, the contact you make may, in time, develop into a major account. It really does make sense to make as many new, personal contacts as possible, and to maximize every opportunity.

Attendance at a meeting of the local chamber of commerce or trade centre can pay dividends in terms of the contacts you may make there. You may even be able to make a presentation (so make sure you have presentation aids such as colour transparencies available).

Knowing your competition is one of the keys to any successful market entry, at home or overseas. This is an ideal time to update your local competitive knowledge. You are physically there in the country, have ready access to local commercial information sources, and can collect competitive data and information much more easily than from home.

You may like to try to develop an 'inside track'; that is, identify a local entrepreneur who wants to make a profit from being your local man or woman. If you are able to identify such a person, and have time to assess them, you may consider it worthwhile to take them on as an information supplier and local market opportunity evaluator in the first instance. An initial small retainer for three months is small money – paid monthly, of course, so that you can get out if they do not generate the business information you need. A likely contender for this sort of appointment is a commercially experienced translator. We deal at more length later in this chapter with the issues involved in appointing agents.

As we have previously recommended, join the local chamber of commerce, where you will certainly make personal contacts and also have access to useful information that could lead you to further contacts and opportunities.

A few key points on developing your sales are as follows.

1 Try to meet as many people as possible, but do be discriminating in whom you spend time with.

2 Do not believe everything you hear.

3 Do visit the outlets of the major competitors in the market. Do not pretend to be a prospective purchaser. If you need more information about them, you will need to appoint someone else to obtain this for you.

4 Always be on the look-out for a prospective business partner, a possible joint venture opportunity, distributor or agent. Good distributors and agents are few and far between – so again cast a wide net and *never* take first offerings for distributorships, partners or agents.

5 Remember that every minute you are present in your new overseas market is a potential business opportunity. Do not waste it. This will require much more work and effort than exploiting the home market.

APPOINTING A REPRESENTATIVE AGENT

The alternative to making direct sales calls or evaluating market opportunities in your export market yourself, is through the formal appointment of a professional, representative agent. In theory such an appointment should consolidate your position. However, there are many pitfalls.

Too many agent appointments are made too hastily, and lack the essential careful process of planning and evaluation needed for any successful appointment. You must take the time to find out about any potential agent. There are many likeable rogues who make quite a good living out of promoting development opportunities for visiting business people, but usually achieve very little for their sponsors.

Many self-styled business promoters, paid only a small retainer, may represent quite a number of companies – some of which may be direct competitors. It is unlikely that they have any real interest in your business. They may supply you with information but it is quite likely not the confidential market information it is purported to be. It may be locally quite generally available (for example from the media or the local chamber of commerce). Agents may supply the same information to different companies and have been known to supply information on one company they represent to another of their clients!

Our advice on the selection of an agent is therefore to exercise great

203

caution and not to be taken in. Given that you are likely to have insufficient time to conduct as thorough an assessment as you would like, we suggest below some tactics to use in questioning a potential agent which should give you some indication of their ability to assist you with your export sales programme. We call this preliminary agent evaluation questioning technique the four 'Put downs'.

1 Lull them into a false sense of security. Encourage them to talk at length about what they have done, the contracts they have arranged, the introductions they have effected. They may even drop some names, enabling you to follow up with a question such as 'I know someone in that company – who were you dealing with?' Any evasive response, or one which breaks client confidentiality is 'Put down No. 1'.

2 Question them closely as to their real knowledge of your market sector. They need to know more than 'buzz words' and snippets from the general trade media if they are to be of use to you. If you conclude that this person does not know about important technical or market issues, this is 'Put down No. 2'.

3 Question them about their knowledge of the competition – their names, position in the market and so on. Have they acted for any of them at any time? If they only know one very well and seem to have up-to-date information, it is quite likely they are still acting for them. Serious lack of knowledge here indicates that they have very little real market experience in your product sector – in their own home market. This is 'Put down No. 3'.

4 What do they know about regulations, legal requirements, health and safety rules, import restrictions or controls, product certification, licence issues or other commercial requirements relating to, or associated with your product or market sector? Most small potential agents are unable to respond directly to such questions. This normally proves that they have never acted for or represented anyone in your market sector. If they had, they would certainly know. If they do not have some reasonable knowledge about these issues this is 'Put down No. 4'.

Regardless of their performance on the above questions, you might just encounter a person with the potential to develop into a most successful agent. If their approach to you is convincing and professional, it is possible that they could use the same skills to promote your products or services.

You will recognize that there is a degree of cynicism in some of our remarks about agent selection. This is deliberate. What you must remember is that, when you are back in your home country you have very little control over an overseas agent. Nevertheless, we would like to conclude this chapter by pointing out that we have known many good agents (both information providers and representative agents) who do give very good value for money, are interested in developing long-term relationships and try to progress good business opportunities for their clients. If you can find a good agent they are very worthy of their remuneration.

An agent, who acts on your behalf to develop contacts and identify sales opportunities rarely becomes engaged in direct selling. Many agents do not have sufficient technical qualifications to promote more complex products or services, or the in-depth sales experience to promote and co-ordinate the sale to point of contract. If you do allow an agent to undertake such obligations, remember that the responsibility lies with you, as the manufacturer or supplier.

In Chapter 17, we turn to alternative methods for developing third party product sale and distribution and discuss the issue of contracts.

THIRD PARTY
DISTRIBUTION

If you only have half an hour to spare on the plane before you land in your new overseas market, you must read this chapter. Almost every export programme starts with some form of agent or distributor arrangement.

AGENTS

We have considered in Chapter 16 some of the benefits and drawbacks of appointing an information or representative agent in your target country of export. A good agent can help you to identify local business opportunities, keep your company profile high with potential customers and prove a valuable source of local information and new prospect acquisition, but you should not expect them to sell your product. They are not your overseas sales representative.

Until the second half of the twentieth century, an overseas business agent was generally perceived as the legal 'in-country' company representative of the 'home country' principal. This was especially true of the shipping industry. Although to some extent agency representation is still valid in law in many countries, the position and status of the agent have changed, particularly since the 1970s. Today, an agent is mainly involved only in business contact development, in identifying and qualifying business opportunities for you, and in maintaining a local 'presence' for your company.

In view of principals' concern about misrepresentation, and apprehension concerning severe financial penalties associated with major commercial error, almost all agents are specifically excluded from becoming the legal representatives of a principal or manufacturer. Thus they have very limited authority to act for and on behalf of their principal.

DISTRIBUTORS

We now look at the selection, appointment, management, direction and control of an overseas distributor.

The benefits of in-country distribution

The selection of a distributor and the commercial arrangements made are the foundation for progressive sales penetration into your new overseas market. The time and effort you invest in the selection process will maximize your sales opportunities within your chosen market, consolidate your market position, considerably raise your market profile and secure your platform for further market exploitation.

For some companies the appointment of a local distributor has been the key to export market penetration, but for others it is a most unpleasant commercial experience involving a total waste of time, resources, effort and money. Indeed, well over 75 per cent of distributor arrangements are discontinued within two years, and very few arrangements last for the life cycle of the product concerned.

Most companies which have failed to develop their export market potentials after appointing a distributor have, however, only themselves to blame. Although many different reasons may be given for the failure of a distributor, most fall within one of the following categories. It is possible to learn, from others' failures, what *not* to do.

1 Those where the manufacturer or principal made an inappropriate decision to appoint in the first place – through lack of experience, training or guidance. More frequently they fail to complete a comprehensive evaluation of the commercial issues or professional evaluation of the competence and technical capability of the distributor.

2 Those where the principals' expectations regarding the distributor's ability to sell the product were unqualified and not based upon factual assessment of local market conditions and opportunity – in terms of both product volume and time scales. In most cases the 'proposed' sales targets were found to be highly over-optimistic. (If sales levels are achieved, distributors' failures in other commercial aspects are often overlooked.)

The price of failure

We have already stated that the failure of a distribution appointment can prove expensive. Now, let us examine some of the potential financial exposures and knock-on effects in more detail.

1 Virtually all the venture capital costs associated with your initial market entry which were incurred in relation to the selection,

appointment and management of the distributor will almost certainly have to be written off. These include all travel and hotel costs, general 'in-country' business expenses, legal or professional service costs – such as translations, financial investigations, lawyers' fees etc. – plus your management and staff time costs associated with this venture.

2 If an arrangement has failed most people will try first to effect a recovery privately with the help of consultants, but such attempts are rarely successful. If the parties are also unable to reach a mutually acceptable discontinuation of the arrangement, there may be no choice but arbitration proceedings or even litigation in a foreign (or your own) country, which is certain to be expensive.

3 The severing of the relationship may have a detrimental effect on the image of your company among potential prospects and your current customers. You may not know what is being said about your company or its products to your current overseas customers from thousands of miles away but you will rapidly see the effect of any such comment in dwindling sales, and the imposition of stronger contractual and financial conditions in any new contracts.

4 Your former distributor should not have too much difficulty securing an appointment with one of your competitors and will almost certainly, regardless of any contracts, non-disclosure agreement or other commercial undertaking made with you, have something of value to offer another principal. For example:

a all of your current and forward prospect list (even if you reach a non-disclosure agreement on this issue, it is almost impossible to prove disclosure);

b a very good appreciation of your product strengths and weaknesses plus a host of technical information;

c your marketing and strategic business plan for local business development, and other valuable information.

There is little point in taking legal action (or going to arbitration proceedings) overseas in such a situation because of the cost – unless the amount of money in contention is very high (say, over US$200 000).

5 If you are involved in engineering, scientific products, technology based systems, products or installations or even white goods, who is going to continue to service and support your customers and installations immediately after the cessation of your current arrangements? If your service and support was provided through your former

distributor, and there is no other service readily available in the region, you face severe problems. Not only could you lose most of your current installed customer base very quickly, but you could also face legal proceedings from present customers for breach of service and support contracts. The cost could be considerable, especially if contracts are medium to long term (two to five years).

Any one of the above exposures could cost you much more than you have spent to date on your total market entry programme. Thus, what might at first seem to be a relatively straightforward matter of terminating a distribution arrangement could expose you to potentially enormous financial and commercial problems. The lesson is clear: careful distributor selection. Nevertheless, regardless of the care you take in your selection procedures, you may still be faced with the need to discontinue a distribution agreement. We therefore strongly recommend that, as a precaution, you incorporate a mutually agreed 'exit route' in your basic distributor agreement or contract.

It is very important, however, never to discontinue any overseas distribution arrangements until you have secured cover for all of the exposures detailed above, by means of firm and fixed alternative arrangements. It always pays to address the 'worst possible scenario' first, and work back from there. At the very least, this will inject an element of caution into your distributor selection and force you at least to consider the consequences of discontinuing any potential or current distribution arrangements.

Appointing a distributor

The selection of a new distributor must evaluate factors in three main areas. These key points are as follows.

1 **Commercial, financial business status and stability.**
2 **Management, administrative, technical, engineering/repair and sales capability to support your product in the market.**
3 **Marketing ability to develop new business, expand your market and sell your product to the agreed volume estimates.**

Note we have placed the 'sales' aspect last – for if you do not get the first two correct, you have little chance of success with sales penetration. We now examine these areas of evaluation in more detail and provide guidelines on each aspect of distributor selection. For each area of

211

evaluation we provide a basic list of questions, to which you may add further questions that are relevant for your market or product sector. Compile all the questions into a pre-prepared, three-section distributor evaluation document, which you may take to distributor selection meetings, and/or formal distributor agreement negotiations.

Some professional overseas market entry consultants allocate points to this process. Points can be useful – particularly when you have to evaluate a large number of potential distributors who appear to be fairly well matched in terms of their ability to sell and distribute your products in your chosen market.

If you wish to use this method of qualification, you will need to weight the points allocated to each area of evaluation in relation to its relevance and importance to your product group and market sector. We recommend that you allocate half of your total points to the area which you have identified as being the most important to you, then allocate the remainder of the points on a pro-rata basis to the other areas in line with your needs. We recommend that you allocate 50 points to the evaluation area most important to you and 20 points each to the two minor areas.

The final element in the distributor evaluation is what we call a 'comfort factor' to which we recommend you allocate 10 points. This covers your overall impressions, your evaluation of the potential business relationship and your own personal observations and instincts.

Some of the factors you might like to take into consideration include the following:

- How you are greeted when you visit their office?
- The state of their premises: are their facilities reasonably clean, neat, tidy and businesslike?
- Have they invested in good quality office technology?
- How do the staff look (happy, bored, overworked)?
- How do they conduct and present themselves in their negotiations and presentations to you? Are they articulate (language difficulties excepted), confident and assured? Are they personally well presented and/or in accordance with local custom/religion?

If you then total all the points, you can calculate the score as a percentage. You do not want a complex computer-based evaluation process requiring much time for the inputting of data and the application of complicated formulae.

This basic evaluation system, although fairly simple, provides a professional, ordered method of conducting the distributor selection process – however many applicants for your distributorship you need to evaluate.

In conducting the assessment you should be prepared to be reasonably flexible. There may well be legal, cultural, historical, or even technical market factors of which you are unaware. For example, if your chosen market requires special attention in such matters as product certification, and you are unaware of this requirement, your weighting of the points could be quite inappropriate. You would then need to further adjust the weighting to take into account this (and any other) issues specific to your product or market sector.

We now examine each evaluation area in turn, and list the questions you need to ask for evaluating potential distributors' suitability.

Commercial and financial stability evaluation

You must make a careful commercial and financial evaluation of your prospective distributor's historical and current business status, that is, you need to seek evidence of reliability, financial and commercial stability and overall good business management sustained over a reasonable period of time.

We now turn to the key questions which should be included in the evaluation of the general commercial status of a business.

Distributor selection: general commercial status review

1 **How long have you been involved in business in this country?** Can you give me a brief historical overview? How long have you been involved directly in our particular market sector?

2 **Which other principals do you represent at present?** May I contact them as a reference?

3 **Do you have a company profile, annual report, audited accounts etc.?** May I have a copy?

4 **How many permanent staff do you employ?** How are they structured? How are your present resources allocated between different principals, representations and distributorships? If you represented us as a distributor what resources would you directly commit to us on a full-time basis?

5 **What commercial references are you able to provide** (suppliers, chamber of commerce, other manufacturers, other representations etc.)?

6 **Are you able and fully qualified to provide direct import commercial support?** This includes import assistance, goods clearance, storage, warehousing, legal documentation, licensing, certification, health and safety compliance, supply chain management and logistics, safety compliance, inspection, insurance, special certificates, customs and excise support, forwarding facilities, barter trade support etc. This list is almost endless: choose only those which have direct commercial application or implication within your product group or service sector. (Please remember – you are not conducting an interrogation.)

7 **Financial matters: are you able to provide bank guarantees and bank references?** Which bank do you use locally and internationally? Within your company and using your current financial arrangements are you able to support bills of exchange, factoring, customer account collections, overdue account management, discount negotiations, finance for stock holding/spares and replacements etc.?

8 **What locations/offices do you have? May I visit?** This is important as a visit will very often give you a 'feel' for the operation. Be wary of short-term rented 'executive' offices in hotel buildings and especially of evasive replies such as: 'It's difficult at the moment as we are in the process of renovation/moving locations etc.'.

9 **What other business interests do you have in this country?** Be very careful how you approach this question as it may be a highly sensitive and/or confidential issue – but of great importance to you. This question is very important if you perceive that your potential distributor has a main stream commercial interest completely outside your specific market sector. The last thing you want is for your company, your products and your business to be right at the end of his/her current priorities list.

10 **Stock issues: will you purchase stock in advance of sale?** If not how do you wish to proceed commercially with stocks of our product? What are your usual/expected 'in-country' customs cleared stock-holding levels?

The above list should enable you to cover most of the main points of a commercial and financial review. Prioritize for yourself the issues which apply more directly to your product or service. If you are unsure of some issues or feel unable to qualify them, a quick informal review of all the above items (completed in a face-to-face interview) will give you an element of security. At least you should then know what they cannot do.

Be tactful in this commercial and financial review. Many people are reluctant to provide detailed financial and commercial information to a virtual stranger, whatever the circumstances. Be reasonable in your requests for information, but remain especially on your guard if you do not receive satisfactory answers or evasion of some of the vital questions on financial matters – especially in relation to references from banks, suppliers and other commercial organizations.

Product and service support capabilities evaluation

You must evaluate the ability of your potential distributor to professionally support your business, and to technically 'underpin' your system, product or service in the market. This is particularly important to you if your product or service is of a highly technical nature.

Many potential distributors will try to maximize their strengths and minimize their weaknesses in responding to your questions in this area of evaluation, in order to appear totally competent in almost every respect, and able to provide the professional product and service support that you require. In reality they often lack some, and perhaps most, of the physical technical support capabilities you consider essential.

You must be aware that you are unlikely to find a potential distributor who fully complies with all of your support requirements. Any distributor who claims to do so is almost certainly exaggerating (or else already represents another similar principal in the market, but has failed to tell you of this).

Representation of more than one principal is not uncommon – especially in developing and third world countries, where the available distributor base is strictly limited. This type of distributor is to be avoided, as their only interest is in obtaining an order and receiving their commission. They have no genuine interest in any one principal's business.

We now turn to the key questions to be asked in order to evaluate the technical and support capabilities of any potential distributor.

Distributor selection: technical and support capability review

1 **Do you currently provide any form of technical service, mainte-nance, repairs or customer support?** For what products? What support do you currently provide within our market sector? How many full-time technical, service or support staff do you employ? What are their qualifications and experience levels with our type of product or service group?

2 **How many field service staff are employed?** Again, ask about experience levels and technical qualifications.

3 **Do you have your own service or repair facility?** May I visit it? If they do not have their own service or repair facility ask how they conduct servicing and repairing at present. Third party service and support poses some difficult issues for complex technical or high technology products. If they are using third party technical support, ask to be introduced to them and visit them.

4 **What spares and repairs stock do you carry as standard?** What sort of volume of stock do you carry for major (regular repair or maintenance) items? How much have you invested in this?

5 **What product or additional technical training will you require in order to support our specific product(s) or service(s) in the local market?**

6 **Are your engineering or support staff technically qualified and able to deal with such issues as pre-installation product testing, major overhauls, accident damage, safety inspection and certification?** If not, how do you deal with these at present?

7 **How many of your current technical or support staff will be allocated to directly support our product(s)?** The distributor may have many technical staff but they are of no use to you if they are all committed to or engaged on other business.

8 **What level of technical (head office) support, training or information are you expecting from me as the manufacturer or supplier?** This is a key question – and often one of the major reasons (other than sales issues) for the distributor–manufacturer relationship to break down. Almost every distributor would like maximum technical support free of charge or at limited cost from the manufacturer or supplier. This substantially reduces the distributor's support costs – and transfers the onus of customer technical ownership and support to

the manufacturer or supplier. It also acts as a general safety net for a distributor if they find that they cannot provide adequate professional support in-country.

Spend a fair amount of time on this question and document full details of support and technical assistance matters which are agreed. Go through the 'Who does what, when, where and to whom' support questions in detail. Carefully document them and always include them as an annexure to your formal distributor agreement. It is very important that both parties have a very clear understanding of their technical and service support responsibilities.

9   **How do you handle returns and repairs to the supplier or manufacturer?** Who pays for it? If it takes considerable shipment time would you require loan stock? What volume of loan stock would you anticipate?

Be very careful about levels of loan or demonstration stock and insist upon strict reporting procedures. There are a number of ways in which distributors can maximize their profits at the expense of a manufacturer or supplier. The first is to return for repair goods that are already out of warranty, claiming that the goods are still covered by warranty. In this way they ensure that the manufacturer or supplier repairs the goods free, and they can charge the customer for repair or replacement. The second ploy involves the use of manufacturer's loan and/or demonstration stock – perhaps renting them out on a short-term basis (and obtaining free repairs under warranty), using them in the distributor's own business, offering them as security against a loan or even selling them.

If you do not have an agreement to receive complete commissioning and installation information, you leave yourself wide open to abuse, additional cost and the possibility of outright fraud. You must regularly check this.

10   **Do you have a quality programme?** Is this formally implemented to international standards (ISO), or is it an in-company programme? May I see some of your quality assurance programme documentation? How do you report faults? What tracking procedures do you use? How do you schedule faults, and what is a typical elapsed time between fault reporting and rectification?

It is very difficult to compile a fully comprehensive list of questions for evaluating technical and support capability, because of the wide variety of issues that need to be addressed. Some matters that are excluded from the above list are customer training, in-country product adaptation, installation planning etc.

However, we believe that the above questions provide a reasonably comprehensive coverage of the major technical support issues which need to be addressed to support technical products or systems overseas. It is always best to seek the advice of your technical or manufacturing director as to the key technical issues to be included.

Sales and new business development evaluation

The third area that must be evaluated – and the one that provides the single major reason for the termination of distributor agreements within the first two years – concerns sales, and the distributor's capability not only to sell your product but to generate further business.

The manufacturer or supplier may have very different expectations of the achievable sales volume from those held by the distributor. Most manufacturers and suppliers have already determined their export sales volume before negotiating with a distributor, on the basis of the calculations and projections incorporated in their original export business plan. Their financial calculations (of cash flow and profit and loss) are in practice unrealistic. For example, they quite often include recovery of all the start-up export costs within a relatively short period (perhaps one year). When translated into equivalent sales revenues (that is, profits) it is almost impossible for most distributors to achieve the necessary returns through high volume sales within the time scale.

Nevertheless, in the rush to sign a distribution agreement, often neither party pays sufficient attention to the determination and qualification of sale revenue expectations. Market conditions vary widely from country to country, as do levels of competitive activity. In addition it is very difficult to calculate distributor sales quotas without long-term local market experience. It is essential to be realistic and practical about sales revenue expectations and expected distributor sales achievement.

We set out below the key questions for qualifying distributor sales potentials so that, together, you and your potential distributor may examine levels of sales expectation.

Distributor selection: sales potential review

1 **How many full-time sales staff do you employ?** What is their geographical distribution? What experience do they have with this type

218

of product or service? Have they received any formal sales and/or product training? Can I go out with one of them tomorrow on some sales visits while I am here?

(Don't allow time for them to set up a special demonstration or untypical sales visit.)

2 **How many of these sales people will be dedicated full time to my product or service?** Will they have individual sales quotas for my product or service? Will they receive commission or special bonus awards for sales of my product or service?

3 **Do you have a sales plan?** May I see it? Will you develop a special sales plan for my product or service? When would I be able to see a draft copy of it?

4 **Do you have a current prospect or identified opportunity list for this type of product or service?** Do you have a prospect evaluation system? May I see it?

5 **Do you have your own marketing programmes?** May I see some examples of them?

6 **How are you going to generate new business for my product or service?** Do you run direct mail programmes, telephone canvassing, exhibitions, seminars, executive briefings? Do your sales people 'cold call'? How do they find new prospects? Do you have any examples of new business generation programmes which you can show me? Do you have a database of potential new opportunities or company lists and/or profiles etc.? May I see them?

7 **Do you have an advertising and/or PR programme?** May I see the schedule? Will you create a special advertising/PR programme for my product or service? How much of your advertising and/or PR budget will you allocate to my product or service? How often do you propose to advertise my product or service? Do you expect me to contribute to your advertising budget? How much would you anticipate this contribution to be for the first year and for second and subsequent years? Will you show me some examples from any of your current advertising campaigns or promotions?

8 **Have you developed any special product or applications portfolios?** May I see one? Do you have product presentation packages or sales kits, overhead foil presentations or videos? Do you have any corporate advertising brochures of your company in your native language? May I see one of them? Are you able to translate manufacturers' or

suppliers' sales brochures, information packs, technical specifications, publicity material? May I see an example of this?

9 **Do you have standard sales order documentation or sales contracts?** May I see one? Do you have any arrangements for third party finance facilities such as leasing or lease/rental to offer to prospective customers? Which company do you have these facilities through, and at what rates? Are the rates fixed or variable? Do you have price books, volume discount tables, special offers? May I see some examples?

10 **What would you expect to be a reasonable annual quota for each of your sales people for my product or service?** What do you think the total overall sales quota should be for the first year of our distribution agreement? How will sales reporting and prospecting for my product be reported to me?

Analyzing sales skills is very subjective, as is the analysis of the overall sales capability of a company. The above list includes not only some very pertinent questions relating to sales structures, coverage, selling capabilities and the ability to identify new business opportunities but also requests for confirmation and qualification. You should assume that if there is no evidence of a capability, it probably does not exist. Do not accept claims without back-up. It is not unreasonable to ask for, or to want to see evidence of present practice. Phrase your questions carefully, and note the answers. If you are unsure about a response, leave it for the present but return to the same question later (phrased differently) to see if you get the same answer.

Remember that the above lists and questions are for guidance only, and should be thoroughly reviewed and amended to suit the requirements of your product or service offering if they are to have any validity as part of an analysis of opportunity. You must try to focus on issues that have particular importance or relevance to your product or market sector. In this way you should be able to create your own distributor evaluation programme.

DISTRIBUTION AGREEMENTS

The next formal stage in distributor acquisition is the preparation, negotiation, agreement and authorization (signing, stamping and sealing) of the formal, legal distribution and representation agreement. The contract is a very important document for both the manufacturer or supplier and the distributor. It sets out in some detail all the legal requirements and commercial expectations for both parties to enable them to develop and maintain a high quality, mutually beneficial, long-term business relationship.

The creation of distribution contracts, which is strictly a legal matter to be dealt with by professionals, is beyond the scope of this book. There are plenty of readily available examples of such agreements. If you do not have your own form of agreement and do not know what to include, you may like to approach some of the multinationals who operate extensive distributor operations, and ask to see a copy of their standard distributor agreement. They are quite often prepared to help other, smaller companies. The distributor evaluation criteria discussed earlier in this chapter should also give you some ideas about what should be included in your distributor agreement.

We provide a few general pointers for drawing up distributor agreements.

1 **One of the most important items to include in the distributor agreement is an agreed exit route for both parties.** If this is pre-agreed and documented, any serious problems further downstream become much easier to resolve.

2 **In many cases initial sales volumes do not reach expected levels.** Regardless of the level at which you agree the sales quota, you must be prepared to revise it. You must include in the distribution agreement an agreed secondary fall-back sales quota level. If even this level is not achieved, you at least have a good benchmark for discussions about the future. Remember that it takes longer to enter and to generate initial sales from an export market than from a home market. You should take into consideration the sales 'ramp-up' (that is, the progressive increase of sales) when you calculate this secondary position. Try to be realistic, and listen very carefully to what your appointed distributor has to say about potential sales volumes. The distributor knows the local market conditions far better than you do. If you want to dictate terms, why appoint a distributor in the first place?

3 **Many potential distributors will try to urge you to enter into a long-term agreement right from the start of your negotiations.** Their claims about the investments they have to make in training, advertising, new business development programmes etc. are valid, but not sufficient. If you do enter into a long-term agreement you may regret it. Try to

convince your selected distributor that a balanced approach is in the best interests of both parties. A distributor must provide proof of their capabilities by developing new business and hard sales resulting in profitable direct sales revenue income. We strongly recommend a one-year agreement as the maximum to begin with. This gives both parties an opportunity to work together on a formal basis, and to evaluate how the relationship is developing. Then, and only if everything is to your mutual satisfaction, should you consider a longer-term agreement.

4 **Any good distributor will always seek rights of exclusivity of representation and/or distribution on your behalf.** (If they do not, you should probably wonder why not.) The decision on whether to grant exclusivity depends upon your approach to your market, your product (exclusivity can be a sales bonus in certain markets, and your company's traditional 'style'. In general, you should always try to avoid granting exclusive rights to sell within a territory, as it is time consuming and expensive to terminate such an agreement if it does not work out.

5 **Your distributor agreement should be quite short, and with the bulk of the secondary issues contained in appendices or supplements.** This format facilitates additions and amendments and saves both parties the need to undertake renegotiation of the agreement.

6 **Dual language agreements are not recommended. If you cannot avoid a dual language document, ensure that it is signed, stamped and sealed by both parties.** Arrange to have the version of the agreement in the distributor's language independently translated by a specialist legal translator and insist that the legal professional who compiled the original document for you in your native language, compares this translation, word for word and line by line, with your original native language document. You may well find some glaring inconsistencies. Even if these are not intentional it is very easy for mistakes to occur in any translation process. These are quite often not grammatical or translation errors, but are caused through the translator's attempts to interpret your meaning when there is no direct equivalent in the other language. Errors of this type very often occur when the agreement contains a large amount of legal terminology. (Hence our advice to keep the main document fairly simple.) The use of legal terminology will not save you from litigation if the agreement founders.

7 **With regard to legal documentation,** very few provincial home country

lawyers have regular and comprehensive experience of international contracts, and even fewer will have experience of the legal system of your chosen country of export. If your market or product sector is such that you might be legally exposed in the future (e.g., through product liability), always have a second set of legal documents prepared by the best 'in-country' international lawyer that you can afford, and ask your own lawyer to cross-check this document.

BUSINESS PLANS AND SALES PLANS FOR DISTRIBUTORS

In developing a distributor's business plan and sales plan you need to adopt the same approach that you used in creating your own business plan for exporting. The sales plan is much more important than the business plan.

Distributor's business plan

The distributor's general business plan should be contained in the distributor agreement. We address this briefly, before we proceed to concentrate on sales.

The distributor's business plan covers all the commercial areas that are not directly sales or marketing issues. Some overlap is inevitable, as it is almost impossible to separate some of the issues. In general, the distributor's business plan sets out the operational guidelines for co-operation between the two parties. It should include terms and conditions of supply, complete pricing and discount structure, together with the technical *modus operandi*.

This business plan is a form of back-up reinforcement to the distributor agreement, but concentrates on agreed methods of working and formalizes business practices, together with the day-to-day business relationships between the parties. An important element is definition of time scales. A procedure without a time scale is easily subject to misinterpretation.

Many arrangements between manufacturers or suppliers and distributors have been successful without an individual distributor's business plan. In such situations, all operational matters, agreed methods of working and time-scale benchmarks must be included in the appendices to the formal distributor agreement. If you are planning a simple but structured, low-cost market entry (Entry 'A') a separate distributor's business plan is hardly worth the additional time and effort. If, however, you are in a complex market sector, have extended sales cycles or are involved with major technology, a separate distributor's business plan will facilitate extended programme planning, provide for project management and a mutually agreed operating plan.

Many people confuse a distributor's business plan with a distributor's sales plan. Sales plans and programmes are absolutely vital to success in overseas markets, and must be reviewed regularly, so please keep them separate. This will enable easy and direct reference to sales issues and will encourage the distributor to concentrate on sales issues – if they have an individual sales plan setting out pre-agreed sales objectives.

Distributor's sales plan

Consideration of the distributor's sales plan is probably the most important part of your export programme. It is the 'make or break' point of all new exporters. Thus this section is the most important part of this book, especially as over 80 per cent of all new exporters choose to use the distributor route for overseas market entry. If you cannot achieve a reasonable volume of sales in your new export market, all your time and effort will have been wasted. Therefore, no effort should be spared to ensure sales success. The keys to this success are firmly embedded in the distributor's sales plan. They are mainly associated with three major sales topics.

1 Sales quotas.
2 Business development programme.
3 Control, direction and management of sales programmes.

Sales quotas

Sales quotas are closely tied to the success of your programme. We consider them in more detail in Chapter 18, so here we provide an overview.

In establishing and setting sales quotas for distributors, you should remember that the quota – regardless of its size – must have four attributes.

1 It must be realistic.
2 It must be reasonably achievable.
3 It must be achieved within a defined time scale.
4 It must be achieved.

Your appointed distributor wants very much to be successful with you, and to make a good income, but does not want to be saddled with an unachievable sales quota. Work with your distributor to determine a realistic and achievable sales target. How you calculate this is for you to decide together. Seek an agreed 'ramp-up' factor for sales – starting small and increasing gradually in line with mutual expectations. If sales are ahead of forecast, you can always increase the quota by mutual consent. These comments underline the importance of professional market research. If the export market opportunity has been qualified and truly exists, you assuredly will sell your product or service. Time spent on research is very rarely wasted, especially if you combine the information you acquire with the latest update from your distributor on prospective business opportunities.

Business development programme

A well structured business development programme is one of the most important means of achieving sales targets. You have already qualified the general market, and have confirmed in theory that opportunities exist for sales of your product or service. However, to bridge the gap between theory and reality, you must engage in an activity-based business development programme.

To maximize sales opportunities you need to generate a new business development programme in close co-operation with your distributor that will ensure that all potential market opportunities are fully covered. To ensure that you achieve the best possible sales results, you require a sales prospect database, compiled in collaboration with your distributor, who knows the local market well. Your distributor needs to know (and to understand) every possible product use and application, type of outlet and any other relevant point that you can remember from your home market. Many of these matters may be applicable in your export market. List them and categorize them by market sector application or product sector. Your distributor should know most of the local sources of information (and if you have done your homework, you should have a very good idea of these yourself). Once you have compiled your database, you need to update and monitor it on a regular basis. Progressive sales penetration in new overseas markets depends heavily upon the quality and size of the potential prospect database.

A structured activity-based sales programme is effective, so long as your product or service is appropriate for such an approach. If it is, follow the formula:

$$\text{CALLS} + \text{DEMONSTRATIONS} = \text{SALES}$$

The sales call may be a canvas call, a fixed appointment or an 'opportunity' type situation. The demonstration may be a hard product demonstration, a presentation, a visit to a reference site – the combinations are numerous. However there is a well-recognized common factor in all of these situations: High sales activity generally brings results.

Regardless of the type of business development programme you finally decide upon, always remember to qualify the individual sales activities with objectives.

Other new business development options, such as advertising programmes, seminars, exhibitions, executive briefings, open days, industry marketing, have a place in a well-structured business development programme. List these as options. Then, on the basis of previous experience and knowledge of local market conditions, decide your best course of action. Having done this, and agreed with your distributor the best sales promotion and development options, write a sub-programme for each type of activity. Bring all of these together in a new business development programme, and write it up as a formal, mutually agreed objective. This final document will then become your mutual new business development programme plan for the next year. Complete this exercise with your distributor. Do not impose a sales development methodology which you know well, or which has been successful in your home market. Talk it through with your distributor, and swap ideas – always trying to ensure that you develop the plan together. You will achieve high personal commitment to success from your distributor if you do it this way.

Before you finalize your programme, seek the opinions of experienced in-country sales staff. They will soon identify any errors.

Management of distributors

Many exporters fail to manage their distributors effectively. The major reason for this is their failure to establish structured reporting procedures for their distributors. Regular, structured reports are necessary, to keep you informed of what is happening in your overseas market and to enable you to achieve direction, control, management and motivation.

Remember, however, that your distributor has agreed to market and support sales of your goods and services in their distribution territory, to pursue mutually agreed business objectives to a satisfactory conclusion. Do not try to run their business or to 'manage' their sales force for them – however tempting it may be on occasions.

The key to a successful partnership with your distributor, particularly with regard to sales issues, is mutual trust and respect. It takes time and effort from both parties to establish this. Successful management of distributor relations depends upon a reasonable degree of continuity of contact, however far away your distributor is.

You should use all the communication methods available to you, depending on the circumstances: personal visit, telephone call, fax, telex, letter and electronic mail. You need to choose the combination of methods that will not only give the quality of communication you require, but also enhance the personal contact element. A combination of electronic mail, telephone and personal visit has proved to be the best, and most cost-effective of combined options in almost all cases. We now address what has to be communicated and with what frequency.

Information exchange

The exchange of information between distributor and principal requires that both parties know exactly where to go for information, what type of information they should acquire and in what format and time scale it should be presented and exchanged.

You should not expect your distributor to present a lengthy monthly business review or report. The distributor could represent a number of principals in different market sectors, and if each of these required a monthly report the distributor would have time for little else than report writing.

The information you need to receive on a regular basis depends a great deal upon your market sector and your product type. If your goods are fast-moving consumer goods you may require daily reports for restocking purposes. If you are involved with products with a long gestation period, such as ships or major civil engineering projects, the reporting time scales are much longer.

In general, your information requirements are of four types.

1 The formal business update. (For most people this does mean some form of monthly report. Try to keep it as short as possible and use a standard format wherever possible.)
2 Technical information.
3 Sales and marketing information,.
4 Business programmes and administration.

A mutually agreed reporting procedure will save much time and effort and prevent many misinterpretations, and you will always have the important information about your overseas business at your fingertips.

Ensure that both your own and your distributor's staff have up-to-date mutual staff contact information, complete with fall-back names. The procedure to supply and update this information should be set up right at the commencement of the distributor relationship.

In the reporting procedure, you should always try to enhance the personal contact element, particularly between technical staff, but with due regard to the costs involved.

Poor distributor performance

It is difficult to manage a distributor at long distance. The best 'management' you can offer them is first-class head office and technical support, with a fast response when they urgently require assistance. The only time that real distributor management should occur is when things are not going according to the agreed plan. Before we discuss how to deal with poor distributor performance, let us examine some of the warning signs to look for.

No one likes to admit that business is bad. Fluctuating sales are easy to justify, but very difficult to rectify. Regular sales tracking – measured against defined and agreed objectives – is the key to overcoming a slide into an unrecoverable situation. Daily, weekly, monthly and even annual variations in sales results can be acceptable, so long as the overall trend is progressively upwards, and the agreed sales objectives are achieved at the end of the year. The major problem is to try to identify, early enough, any splippage against sales plan that will be difficult to recover in the short to medium term. For example, if there are not sufficient prospects or sales qualified in the forecast for the next month (or the next three months) to bring you back on plan you will soon find yourself with a backend-loaded sales forecast. (Backend loading occurs when, each month, you progressively fall behind the sales target and add the deficit to future months in the hope of making up the deficit later and achieving the total year's target by the end of the year. This is very difficult to achieve. Therefore, any trend or indication towards backend loading should prompt you to action.)

Some other signs of distributor under-performance include additional requests for greater technical or sales support, delay in settlements, 'padded' prospect lists, the drying up of information and delay in sales reporting. A rapidly declining prospect list is the most obvious indicator.

Take heed of the warning signs and take action. The problems will not disappear on their own. What steps you take will be governed by your market and product sector. You should discuss the situation with your distributor, agree that there is a potential problem, develop a rectification programme together, then let your distributor implement it. A prudent overseas market developer will always have a few additional sales promotion programmes available for such situations. It is important that the rectification programme be implemented quickly. The situation can quickly deteriorate further, especially if the distributor utilizes your resources to promote other manufacturers' products that can earn better financial rewards with less work. The more closely you work with your distributor, the less likely this is to happen.

AN EXIT ROUTE

We have already stated that one of the most important issues to be covered in the distributor agreement is the identification, agreement and documentation of an exit route for both parties, as a last resort. You should discuss this possibility at the beginning of the distributor relationship, ensuring thereby that you safeguard service and support arrangements.

It is difficult to have to admit to the failure of a distribution arrangement, but if an agreed series of professional rectification measures have been implemented and have not achieved any substantial turn-round, it is necessary to recognize that the situation is irrecoverable and the arrangement should be terminated before further losses occur.

In terminating an agreement, always try to part on good terms. Anger and animosity are of no use. Furthermore, there may be future opportunities to collaborate, for example if the market changes, a major competitor withdraws, significant cultural change occurs, or you have a new or enhanced product. Always leave the door open – regardless of the location of the market. If you fail to achieve your objectives, you should still be able to learn from the experience.

EXPORT SALES QUOTAS AND TARGETS

INTRODUCTION

The determination of distributor sales quotas underpins your total overseas market entry programme in terms of business volumes, and is fundamental to overall market entry success. Nevertheless, most aspiring exporters fail to achieve a well balanced and practical sales plan with their distributors or agents. As the overall failure rate for sales plan achievement is so high, and this is such a critical part of any overseas market entry programme, we devote the whole of this chapter to this topic.

By far the greatest single reason for the failure to achieve the distributor or agent sales plan is that the targets were set too high. Furthermore, insufficient consideration is given to establishing realistic baseline quota projections from which to establish a 'ramp-up' of sales over time.

We strongly recommend you to set a slightly low quota for the first year. As we pointed out in Chapter 17, a quota must be achievable. Success in achieving the target at the beginning generates confidence in your product or service on the part of your distributor's sales people. It is then possible to raise the target and progressively ramp up sales.

This approach to the determination of distributor sales targets will not only generate faith in, and commitment to, your product by your distributor, but, through initial target achievement, assist in confirming the viability of the product in the market. Although this approach does not exploit fully every available opportunity by imposing pressure upon sales staff with high targets, it is the proven best sales policy for the first year of overseas market entry.

Given that there are bound to be a number of programme implementation and operational problems during the first year, it is wiser to have the time and resources to address these issues professionally than to be unable to do so because of constant pressures to achieve high sales targets.

A third reason for setting lower initial targets is that it gives both you and your distributor the time to professionally implement high quality sales and marketing programmes, and to undertake comprehensive product training. Good quality sales and business generation programmes will ensure that you cover all of the major product opportunities. You will miss out on very few sales by setting an initial reduced quota. If the distributor's sales staff are well trained to sell the product (or service), make all of the necessary sales calls, and work hard at developing new business, you will almost certainly achieve most of what the market will stand anyway.

It is well recognized that within almost all sales environments, to achieve the last 10 per cent or 20 per cent of sales target usually requires far more time and effort than to achieve the previous 80 per cent of target. Do you really want to handicap your new distributor by setting an unrealistic target and forcing him/her to expend disproportionate effort to achieve the last 10 per cent of available business in the first year? It is better to be realistic, and recognize the value of having a motivated distributor, with sales and technical staff keen and committed to achieving success. No one likes management pressure, especially when they are dealing with a new market sector or product. Allow some time for the learning experience to take place.

DETERMINING SALES QUOTAS AND TARGETS

Many manufacturers and suppliers have little idea of how to calculate sales quotas and targets for new export markets.

We now provide some guidelines for determining a realistic and accurate sales target for your first year of operation in your new overseas market. Your records of sales volumes in your early trading days in your home market may provide some indication of the 'inhibiting' factors which you had to face in your home markets, and the sales records for that period should give you some idea of the level at which to set the quota.

It is at least twice as difficult to develop a new business in a far distant country as in a home market. The logistics and long-distance implementation problems incurred in overseas operations alone reinforce this statement. From the records of your first year's sales in your home market, determine the approximate number of sales achieved by the product which is to be your lead export product, then divide this number by 2 and file it away for later reference. This number will be a reference to check against when you have completed a professional evaluation of the level of opportunity in your export market.

We present the methodology for sales target calculation in the form of a real-life example taken from an exercise we completed for a manufacturer of white boards.

■ White board exports

An office supply manufacturer had been interested in a particular export market for some time, when an opportunity arose enabling him to take some time away from his current business commitments to develop an export programme. He followed many of the programmes contained in this book and completed a comprehensive market survey, together with quite a professional competitive and market opportunity analysis, and calculated a reference figure for first year's sales (as explained on the previous page). Finally he needed to set the first year's sales quota.

Opportunity analysis

The first task was to determine the overall potential market size. We thought about who uses white boards and where. Most businesses could use one, but by no means all businesses – you don't see many white boards in retail shops, for example. Other potential customers include offices, schools, colleges, universities, research establishments, sales departments and even taxi cab firms (for listing waiting customers). We made as comprehensive a list as possible.

We now attempted to quantify the market, always trying to support the numbers with qualified independent statistics. For example, if you wish to know the total number of businesses in a country you should consult the Central Office of Statistics or the Department of Business Registration or even a chamber of commerce, which can usually provide you with that information easily. Wherever possible you should try to list this information by industry sector using the SIC (Standard Industrial Classification) numbers. This will help you to identify the key areas of opportunity quickly, and makes for a more accurate projection overall.

We made some logical assumptions.

1 As a white board has a considerable physical lifetime, we must assume that in most cases only one unit will be purchased per office – and will last for many years.

2 We also assume that some identified and qualified establishments would be capable of purchasing at least two units. (Have you ever seen a multinational or a research establishment with only one white board?)

3 Finally, we assume there are some specific types of business which do not normally use a white board. (You do not see many garages, retail shops or bars with a white board.)

We then compiled an exceptions list and assumed zero returns. After this we began to compile our data. Some examples are given in Table 18.1.

Table 18.1 Opportunities for sales of white boards

Business type	No. of opportunities	Multi-sales opportunity factor	Total opportunities
Schools	2 000	× 1	2 000
Multinationals	55	× 2	110
Offices	4 000	× 1	14 000
Research establishments	100	× 2	200

Table 18.1 provides a reasonable basic estimate of the total market opportunity for white boards.

There were 27 000 industry-coded potential customers in the total market. We had to reduce this total by the numbers already sold by the competition. In this case, the competition was not well established: it was fairly thinly spread across a broad cross-section of market sectors and industry types. (If you want to assess overall market size in greater depth, use sampling techniques to back up your conclusions. Take a random group of five major potential outlet types and visit a few of them: you will soon get some indications.) In this instance the market for white boards was not very well penetrated (with only local supply through several small retailers of office equipment) and we estimated that less than 25 per cent of the total available market had been exploited.

Our calculation of 27 000 less about 25 per cent indicated about 20 000 potential opportunities to sell white boards. As the selling price was around $100 per unit and the average margin 30 per cent, this represented well over half a million dollars of profit opportunity.

With a total market opportunity in excess of 20 000 units over a period of at least five years, we then had to convert this statistic to target or sales quota projections. If our client was to become a major supplier in the market (we did not say dominate the market at this stage) we would expect them to achieve at least 33 per cent of the potential market over the next five years. This was the base line calculation for the estimated total number of qualified potential sales over the next five years – without any expansion factor.

We hoped that they would be able to significantly improve upon this number. The above basic analysis indicated that there was a potential sales volume of around 7000 units over a five-year period. To this base line number, we then needed to add a market expansion factor. As the rate of growth of registration of new businesses over the previous five years (a figure obtained from the Department of Trade) had averaged 2 per cent per annum, rounded up, this equated to approximately 15 per cent compound growth over a five-year period. So we calculated that we could expect around 1000 additional units of qualified market opportunity through new business registrations. This brought us to an estimated figure of at least 8000 units over the next five years. With a reasonable sales and marketing programme we calculated that our client should become a major player (with over 33 per cent of the market) in this time.

The 8000 units (straight line projection) divided by 5 years gave 1600 units per annum. This was not the figure to use to set the first (and subsequent years') sales targets. We needed to identify a realistic but progressive set of achievable projections. A rule of thumb for this is to calculate the 'ramp-up' of sales over a five-year period based on the percentages given in Table 18.2 (all figures rounded up for convenience).

Table 18.2 Sales projections over a five-year period

Year	Percentage of total five-year potential	No. of units
1	6.25	500
2	12.5	1000
3	18.75	1500
4	25.0	2000
5	37.5	3000
Total	100.00	8000

Clearly, the sales target for year 1 of 500 units was significantly below the average (i.e., the original straight line projection of 1600 units per annum). It was not until the start of the third year that sales would begin to approach this average number of 1600 units.

You will find it useful to carry out a similar exercise to the above on your home market sales.

Market forecasting, at its best, is rather an inaccurate science. There are so many variables, beyond simple product or market sector analysis, that it becomes almost impossible to produce consistently accurate quota targets, even with computer modelling techniques. The above example is a basic structured approach to determining reasonable and realistic sales targets, rather than a detailed scientific analytical evaluation. In following this example you will at least have some estimates which bear a direct relationship to your product and market. You will therefore give your distributor some confidence that you are prepared to make an evaluation based on local data, rather than to impose a quota which fits nicely into your financial business plan.

PROSPECT IDENTIFICATION

One of the benefits of calculating sales quotas is that it forces you to consider who can use or purchase the product or service, and when and where. This gives you a reasonable local market profile. (You also know where not to go to try and generate new business prospects.)

Prospect identification and qualification is a basic requirement of any business that wishes to be successful and wishes to earn good revenues. The key word is qualification. One qualified prospect is worth ten pages of a general prospect list.

THE ACCOUNT STRATEGY AND PLANNING SYSTEM

We are now going to take you through a part of our account strategy and planning system (ASPS). This system is covered elsewhere, so here we look only at a section of the ASPS dealing with the process of qualifying export market prospects. The ASPS process will greatly assist you in maximizing sales potential, whatever your product, market sector or geographic location.

ASPS PROSPECT QUALIFICATION

The ASPS prospect qualification process depends largely on categorizing prospects within pre-defined and carefully selected parameters. For the sake of clarity we review only the main ASPS prospect categories and provide some indicators of how to proceed with prospect qualification.

All prospect evaluations and qualifications need clarification. To establish an accurate prospect list you must ask such questions as: Is it a real prospect or isn't it? If it is, how good a prospect is it? What do I need to do next? When can I realistically expect to close the order?

The first step in professional prospect evaluation and qualification is to determine the average time scale for an order. This time scale is measured from the first point of contact with a prospect or potential customer to the time at which you receive a signed contract or order.

(Note that 'being paid' is not part of the ASPS prospect qualification process. This belongs to ASPS account management.)

The order time scale can vary enormously – depending upon product type, complexity, market sector, and many other variables. Regardless of the mix of variables, you should have a reasonable idea of the sales time scale from your experience of home market sales. Shops and retail premises often measure sales time in terms of days – particularly if the product is classified as Fast-Moving Consumer Goods (FMCG) (especially food). Other market sectors and organizations measure the time scale in weeks, business-to-business sales in months, and those involved in long-term projects like shipbuilding or major telecommunication projects, in years.

Regardless of your product type, calculate a realistic average based on current available information and then add 20 per cent to allow for export market factors such as translation of quotations or bids, additional time required to receive technical information from home market head office, and other similar delaying factors. (We have found 20 percent to be a good average for non-specialist products. If your product is specialized you may need to adjust the percentage accordingly.)

Having established your product sales cycle time, continue with the prospect qualification process. A sales prospect may be qualified in many different ways. You should aim to establish a common understanding between everyone involved in the sales and business management process as to where each prospect is within its specific sales cycle (and its status). If you are then able to apply a time scale factor you should have a much clearer understanding of your prospect list and be able to determine, with some degree of accuracy, the volume of potential sales and when they will occur. In addition, when you apply these factors to the ASPS process, you will also generate a 'What to do next' list to further promote every sales opportunity. This facilitates good understanding between all sales staff and sales management and promotes good quality account management to the point of achievement of the sale.

The next stage in prospect qualification is to break down the sales cycle into qualified areas classified from A to E, with those at the beginning of the sales cycle classified as 'E' and those that may be considered immediate business opportunities classified as 'A'. The examples provided below may have to be adapted and modified to suit your specific product or service, but we have never yet found any product or service offering which is incapable of being rated using this method.

'E' category prospects

The 'E' prospects should be considered your 'call forward' list of identified prospect opportunities. Every known and identified potential prospect should be included in the 'E' category, regardless of its status or the amount of information known about them. The only qualifier is that you have a strong and confirmed belief that this is the type of prospect which has the capability to buy your product.

Only your experience with your product or service will enable you to decide who should, or more importantly who should not, be included as an 'E' category prospect. The 'E' category potential prospects are those whom you have not yet contacted to instigate a formal sales process.

The 'E' list is the bedrock upon which all sales success is built. If the 'E' list is poorly selected, and very brief, you will have little chance of achieving good sales volumes. (This statement does not apply to highly specialized products or niche markets.)

'D' category prospects

Concentrating on the process rather than a specific product or service market, we define a 'D' category prospect as one who has completed an ASPS profile. (The ASPS profile contains, in addition to all the base information regarding company name, address, contact numbers, initial contact names etc., such information as current type of product or equipment used, types of system or processes in which the product or service is employed, and an initial evaluation as to whether your product or service is saleable to that company.)

A 'D' category prospect is one whom your sales staff have contacted either by telephone, or personal visit (not by letter, telex or fax), and for whom they have made an individual basic assessment as to the potential for that person or company to buy your product or service.

'C' category prospects

A 'C' category prospect will have completed an ASPS review. For an ASPS review to take place, your sales staff must have formulated a sales approach or sales programme to penetrate that account and initiate a formal sales process. A 'C' category prospect is one whom your sales staff have visited, by appointment, who has received brochures and technical information and who has perhaps even been taken to a 'reference' customer's office, site or location. A 'C' category prospect is qualified as being quite well educated about your product or service. Agreed needs will have been established and confirmed with a 'C' category prospective customer.

'B' category prospects

A 'B' category prospect is one to whom much more specific criteria are applied – not only in terms of in-depth qualification of likelihood of buying the product, but also in terms of the likely time scale.

A 'B' classification prospect may be considered as one where an order is probably closable within about three months. (You must determine your own time scales for this. It does not matter much if your initial estimates are not entirely accurate, as you will be able to refine this figure as you compare it against a number of closed orders over time.) Additional criteria are attached to a 'B' category prospect which formalize the sales process and its relationship to the prospect. For example, you would wish to see that your sales staff have prepared and presented a proposal, quotation, and other such sales materials to the prospect for their consideration. If applicable, the product should have been demonstrated and a key Need-Feature-Benefit list should have been generated. Your staff will also have confirmed that the prospect has the financial resources to pay for the product or service. You need to pay close attention to your specific product or service offering, and to include all those key factors which past experience has shown to be essential to progressing the sale. These include general sales progression and prospect enhancement factors such as the provision of third party finance, rental or lease options, project management plans, or implementation programmes, site surveys, connectivity issues, detailed overviews of the major applications. Many of these items are product or market specific.

'A' category prospects

'A' category prospects represent your immediate business opportunities. A specific time scale should be attached to them, such as, for example, 'closable' within one month. Your sales staff will have carried out the necessary steps to ensure that an 'A' category prospect has completed all the formal sales processes. Your staff will have identified and made contact with all of the known decision influencers or decision makers. They will have ascertained (as closely as possible) the date when the order decision will be made, and will have confirmed that a budget has been drawn up or other financial provision has been made. In broad terms an 'A' category prospect is as close as possible to becoming a customer without an order being signed – the only thing needed is a purchase decision. Your sales, technical and other staff involved in the sales process should have completed to a high degree of competence all of their individual parts of the sales process. For a potential customer to be classified as an 'A' category prospect, it is also necessary that there has been a formal presentation of your product or service to the key decision makers in the organization, and that no step that would assist the purchase decision has been omitted. Now is not the time to discover that the customer does not have any available budget allocation.

If you have carefully defined the parameters of the 'A' category prospect classification and related them closely to your own product or service, your sales close ratio with 'A' category prospects should be very high. (A sales close ratio is the number of sales you close against a number of qualified prospects. For example, if you have 100 qualified prospects and close 20 of them your sales close ratio is 5 to 1.)

Using the ASPS prospect qualification procedure

The most important aspect of the ASPS prospect classification process is defining the prospect categories as precisely as possible in relation to your product or service. Once you have developed and implemented your own qualification process for your prospects, all staff – both yours and those of your distributor – should have a common understanding of what is meant by, for example, a 'B' category prospect: where such a prospect fits in the sales process, and the importance of the sales opportunity it presents.

The ASPS prospect qualification and classification methodology may be further developed to provide sales forecasts. We have regularly achieved sales results of between plus and minus 15 per cent against forecast based upon ASPS. Over a long time scale, results of between plus and minus 20 per cent are regarded as good.

As explained earlier in relation to the classification of prospects into categories, your knowledge of average sales cycle times for your product(s) should enable you to establish average sales close ratios and time scales, from which you should be able to develop a process that will statistically project, with some accuracy, the likely number of sales (overall and within each prospect category) in a given time. Your forecast should be reasonably accurate because it is based upon pre-qualified data.

Further refinement of sales close ratios, and prospect list qualification is, of course, possible and useful, but may contribute only marginally to overall sales achievement within your overseas markets. The essential requirement is good prospect account information as a baseline from which to make assumptions.

As we close this chapter we would like to reinforce and emphasize again the importance of developing customized and qualified prospect classifications. In order to have control over sales forecasting, you and your distributor must know the true status of your current prospect list. You will then be able to spot downward trends, leading to poor sales performance, and will have time to effect recovery.

Chapter

19

DIRECT REPRESENTATION IN EXPORT MARKETS

INTRODUCTION

The previous two chapters cover the two major methods of indirect export market entry through the appointment of an agent or a distributor. The major disadvantage of indirect market entry is the lack of control over the operation of the other party. However good your control systems, the working relationship, the reporting system, your sales promotion materials etc., you cannot be sure that sufficient effort is going in to promoting your sales and products.

The lack of direct control, and reservations regarding day-to-day performance, have persuaded many exporters to seek alternative arrangements for the promotion of their goods or services in export markets. This chapter examines one form of direct representation, the appointment of a resident regional sales manager. Chapter 20 examines other forms of direct and indirect representation.

APPOINTING A RESIDENT REGIONAL SALES MANAGER

The appointment of a resident regional sales manager (RSM) begins with a definition of their key functions.

Key functions of a resident regional sales manager

1 The RSM must promote our goods or services in the best possible manner and achieve a good sales result for us.
2 The RSM will be responsible for all market development, sales promotion and technical requirements to support the business.

The above should be achieved at the lowest possible cost, and within a pre-agreed time scale. In relation to the appointment itself, you must decide what type of person you need: primarily a technical person or a sales person. If the latter, do you need a representative whose major function is calling on buyers, or a creative sales person to sell the 'idea' or concept of your product or service? Clearly, the sales requirement is the most important issue. The RSM is there to *sell*.

Your home market experience with your products or services should guide you as to the type of sales person you should recruit. We list below some other (export market) considerations.

Key qualities in a resident RSM

1 **Language.** If the language of your export market is not your native language, your RSM must be truly bilingual, and preferably a native (native speaker) of the country. You do not want to have to pay translators, or drivers to act as guides. Nor should you expect a non-speaker of the language to learn it 'on the job': this wastes time and reduces the selling efficiency of the appointee.

2 **Technical ability.** If your product or service is of a technical nature it may be very important that your RSM has relevant technical skills. If you cannot find anyone with these skills, you should be able to train them, even though this will take some time.

3 **Computer skills.** The RSM should have basic PC skills including knowledge of spreadsheets.

4 **Approach to costs.** If you are working to a tight budget you should select someone who wishes to grow with the business and who is prepared to take a professional view of costs in the early days, in order to minimize overheads and operating costs (including remuneration and benefits).

5 **A self-starter.** Your RSM must be reliable and a self-starter. The comments at the start of this chapter concerning indirect management and control also apply to a resident RSM. The appointee is a member of your staff, but you must be confident that your RSM will be totally devoted to your business.

Managing the appointment process

You should advertise the RSM position in the major national newspapers of your export country – both in a paper published in your own language and in one published in the local language. (If there is no paper published in your language, choose the English-language paper.) The advertisement should be in your home country language to ensure that you receive responses from bilingual applicants.

If you have any doubts about your personnel selection skills seek the assistance of a local recruitment agency, or staff selection bureau.

Although professional personnel selection procedures should enable you to appoint the right person, there is an element of risk and you should if possible stipulate a trial period of employment and also make provision for termination of the appointment if this becomes necessary.

COSTS

The appointment of a resident RSM involves considerable costs. Both salary and overhead costs will be much higher than for an agent or distributor. You can save on overheads, at least in the short term, by appointing as RSM a person who is prepared to work from home – at least for the first year. This saves the cost of office rental plus other setting-up costs, which are extremely high in most capital cities. There are complex procedures, entailing considerable legal costs, for setting up an overseas operation (discussed in Chapter 20) and these may be avoided by the appointment of an RSM.

The RSM will need office equipment and supplies. You may be able to supply these items from head office. The minimum equipment includes a PC system incorporating a dual-language keyboard, an e-mail connection and software for producing full-colour materials (such as sales quotations, proposals, bids, product sheets and presentation aids such as foils and transparencies); a colour printer (with a font set in the local language); a fax machine; a telephone answering machine; and perhaps a small copier but this may not be necessary as copy volumes are usually quite small. The total cost of the above should be approximately US$5000 (1997 costs). Your RSM should not need ancillary staff, at the beginning, although, in some environments, a driver may be useful.

You should also budget for the cost of bringing your new RSM to spend some time in your home country head office for familiarization or product training.

INDUCTION OF A NEW REGIONAL SALES MANAGER

Regardless of whether your product or service has technical content for which training is required, your new RSM should spend at least a few days at head office. The visit provides an important opportunity for both you and your staff to develop a personal relationship with the new RSM. Ensure that all your staff realize the importance of the appointment and know of the impending arrival of the RSM. Plan and conduct a full induction programme, so that the new RSM becomes familiar with your organization and products and meets key members of your staff. The 'bonding process' is particularly important for the future relationship between the RSM and your key export staff. If time is available, arrange entertainment and opportunities to see something of your country and culture.

Ensure that your RSM receives all the items they perceive as necessary to support the business.

Before the RSM completes the familiarization visit, ensure that all communication or other problems associated with long-distance RSM management have been resolved. Ensure that the new RSM has a clear understanding of what is required – not only in terms of achievement of targets and sales results but also in terms of frequency and content of communications, business development programmes, prospect development, account strategy, export market and competitive analysis information and strategic export plan development. Any problems or misunderstandings will be more difficult to resolve at a distance.

Because your RSM operates at long distance entirely on their own, they need qualities of enthusiasm and positive thinking which you must help them to achieve.

MONITORING THE PERFORMANCE OF A REGIONAL SALES MANAGER

We now turn our attention to RSM performance monitoring. Effective communication is the key to managing distant employees. Performance monitoring and evaluation should be conducted weekly. It is not adequate to rely on a monthly report. By the time a problem is highlighted in the monthly report it is almost already too late. All too often the monthly report bears little or no resemblance to the real situation. This situation cannot develop if your monitoring is adequate.

To improve the monitoring of overseas performance and evaluation of business development, you need an export manager – or perhaps an export 'co-ordinator' – in your home country head office. Use e-mail to maintain regular contact and try to develop an informal but consistent communications approach. Effective daily communication is necessary. Both you, and they, will soon get used to this discipline, and it will become a normal and expected part of their daily routine. The monthly report does have its place, but it is no substitute for regular informal communication. If you keep the daily communication informal you will provide the consistent support that is so necessary in developing long-distance relationships. It will also improve RSM motivation.

REMUNERATION OF A REGIONAL SALES MANAGER

To motivate your new RSM, you must provide fair remuneration, including bonus and sales commission. Before you pay any bonus or commission you want to receive something. In return, however, you should not always gear bonus payments directly to sales results. There are many other achievements, especially in the early days, which could (and should) be rewarded by a bonus. These include the creation of a good quality prospect list and (often overlooked) success in operating within the allocated budget. If you can encourage your RSM to spend their budget allocation as if it were their own money, you will have a good measure of export budget control.

Every company has their own type of sales compensation scheme. If appropriate, your home market bonus scheme can be implemented in your export market. This has the benefit of simplicity of administration and speedy implementation. You should agree commission terms at the time of appointing your new RSM – and certainly not later than their departure from their familiarization visit to your home country head office. Nothing is more demotivating for a sales person than not to know their sales commission terms.

Regardless of the type of sales commission scheme you implement, it has to be reasonably achievable. If you want to maximize the potential motivation provided by any sales commission plan ensure that your commission scheme contains at least the following elements.

Key elements of a sales commission scheme

1 **Realistic targets.** Start with a fairly low (achievable) target, and build on this.
2 **Reward regular achievers.** Give a 'rolling' quarterly bonus which enables people to catch up. This ensures maximum continuity of effort to win sales.

3 **Annual bonus.** Save some of the sales commission budget for allocation as an additional year-end bonus, geared to the successful achievement of total quota or total target for the year.

4 **'No limit' sales commission scheme.** Do not revise targets or implement ceilings in response to a substantial sale. One person who achieves 200 per cent of target makes the quota of two people at almost half the cost of two people.

5 **Consider local factors.** There may be particular (local) reasons for failure to secure immediate commission payments. For example, in some countries it is accepted business practice for payments for goods or services to be slow. Your scheme may stipulate that sales commission is only paid when payment is received, but it may not be fair or reasonable to make an employee who has worked long and hard to achieve a sale wait months before being paid commission. Such schemes do protect the company but they do not provide much motivation. A good compromise in overseas markets is part-payment of commission on order. This largely protects the company's interests. Try to include a 'recoverable' factor to protect yourself in the event of major default with a confirmed and qualified customer order. Be very careful with large export orders and have a separate (stricter) sales (and commission) administration procedure.

6 **Pay promptly.** If you can gear payment of commission and bonus directly to the previous month's sales performance, pay it regularly and pay it on time; you will motivate and earn great respect from your sales people.

7 **Prevent manipulation of bonus/commission schemes.** It is very difficult to deal with all the ways in which staff may try to secure additional commission (e.g. by rescheduling of orders to catch up). The sales plan bonus and commission scheme documentation should be as comprehensive as possible, but should not include a catch-all clause like 'The Company reserves the right at all times, for whatever reason, to withhold payment of commission.' This is a sign of weak management, lacking in business confidence and sales plan professionalism. You already have implemented strict controls regarding major orders – that should be more than sufficient for the present.

8 **'Freezing' commission.** Always reserve the right to 'freeze' commission or bonus payments to staff who have handed in their notice. This is normal accepted practice in sales environments.

In conclusion, you should recognize that the appointment of your own resident RSM is a significant milestone in your overseas market entry programme. Although the costs of appointing an RSM are not very different from those of a successful distributor receiving commission of 25–40 per cent, the bonus is the fact of having your own RSM resident in your export market focusing on your products – all of the time.

Chapter 20

OTHER BUSINESS
CONSOLIDATION
OPTIONS

Instead of appointing an agent, a distributor or a resident regional sales manager, you may effect market entry and consolidation by other means. This chapter reviews a number of diverse, but related alternatives. These include direct operations or indirect ventures.

1 Direct (wholly owned) subsidiary company.
2 Partnership.
3 Joint venture (with or without manufacturing facilities).
4 Operating agreement.
5 Licence agreement.
6 Franchise.
7 A combination of the above.

SUBSIDIARY COMPANY OPERATIONS

Establishment

The establishment of subsidiary company operations entails some degree of risk, and a reasonably complex legalization process. The simplest form is the registration of a representative office, or a low-cost general business registration. The requirements (and the costs) vary from country to country, so – regardless of your qualifications and experience – you should seek local legal and financial advice regarding the procedures for registration, legalization, regulatory requirements and so on.

Once the registration process is completed you will need advice on the selection of premises, staff, equipment, IT systems, communications systems and specialists such as forwarding agents, customs agents, bankers and other professional advisers.

Consolidation

Only companies with substantial financial resources and experience of the market should consider establishing overseas subsidiary operations. Many overseas market failures include companies which committed themselves to subsidiary company operations, when they would have been wiser to embark on a low-cost progressive market entry pro-gramme, with each stage being qualified and confirmed before proceeding further. The fact that major multinationals have succeeded in establishing a subsidiary operation in a particular country is no indica-tion that you will succeed in your market sector.

Subsidiary company formation is a high-budget, high-cost business project requiring full preliminary evaluation. There is little margin for error and mistakes can lead to substantial financial loss, with a severe impact upon your overall corporate profits. There are many hidden costs, such as those related to regulatory matters and time scales, to be identified, addressed and budgeted for.

Your company's performance in the home market, and particularly in effecting market entry, is one indicator of future performance overseas. However, if a market expansion opportunity is proven to exist, it is almost certain that other companies will also have recognized it. Boldness has its virtues, as the first major player in the market quite often secures the largest proportion of the available market. You should there-fore give the appearance of being very confident – even if you are not.

Although the formation of an overseas subsidiary, which is a major business expansion step, will give you the sales, technical and adminis-trative capability to capture the market, you have to be sure (through extensive research or preferably by pilot low-cost entry) that a market with expansion potential does exist. It is important that any advice you seek for evaluating this potential be wholly unbiased. The majority of business consultants are totally professional but you should be aware that there are some advisers, for example, local insurers, PR companies, who may have a vested interest in recommending market entry.

Many companies choose to commission a professional evaluation of market potential. Although the quality of most consultancy reports is high, we must point out that not all achieve the same standard. Some are poorly structured, lack accuracy and meaningful content and have been compiled by inexperienced researchers with no real understanding of local market factors or conditions. These researchers – often part-time university students – have little or no understanding of your overall business objectives or of the potential exposures with which you could be faced.

Much of the material in such reports is not original (particularly the background information) and is simply readily available commercial information presented in the form of a personalized report.

You should think very carefully before commissioning an evaluation of market potential. However, there are some technical fields, such as mining, gas and oil exploration, where such an evaluation is always considered necessary. We set out below the key issues you should review before commissioning any consultancy or 'specialist' evaluation.

1 **What real (proven) experience or exposure does this consultancy company (specialist) have within my market sector?**

2 **What local presence, and more particularly, specific local market sector experience does it have in my targeted country of export?**

3 **Is it able to provide me with a reference list of previous (similar) assignments which I can contact independently?**

4 **Who will be professionally responsible (full time) for my project?** Insist on having a full-time partner in direct control and management of your consultancy project on a day-to-day basis.

5 **What guarantees of the accuracy of the report's findings and conclusions are offered – specifically in regard to any recommendations for action?** This is a difficult and often highly contentious area, as very often a consultant wishes to act purely in an advisory role, and disassociate themselves from any form of responsibility for the outcome of their findings or recommendations. If consultants were contractually obliged to implement their recommendations, their reports would be much more highly qualified.

We strongly recommend that you conduct your own pilot market entry programme yourself. This will obviously be cheaper than employing a professional, and – by using the procedures outlined in this book – you will obtain an unbiased evaluation of the potential market.

It is conservatively estimated that the minimum investment (in 1997) for establishing an overseas subsidiary operation is US$200 000. This figure does not include the cost of an independent consultancy report or of the additional time factor incurred. If you consider what indicators of success you would seek before committing to such an investment for your home market expansion, you will realize the wisdom and cost-effectiveness of a trial market entry programme. With a minimum base cost of around $200 000, and a gross profit to turnover ratio of 1 to 5, you would need to achieve a minimum sales turnover of at least $1m to break even on market entry costs, never mind operating costs or an extended financial recovery period.

If your operation is likely to require considerable technical support, a large amount of stock or demonstration equipment, or involves perishable goods (which could incur considerable stock losses), be very cautious. If you are involved in a high-tech market sector and may require licences or product certification, be even more cautious. You may need to add at least 50 per cent to cover these additional requirements. You need to be aware of these potential costs at the beginning, and to include them in your financial projections. Once the subsidiary company is in operation, it is too late to revise your business plan. If faced with the requirement to make a major payment in order to comply with, for example, licensing certification or of safety regulations, the alternative to paying is to drop the project – at a significant loss.

If you try to save money by bending the rules, or by avoiding or ignoring legal, financial, technical or safety obligations, you will eventually be found to be acting illegally, or in contempt of local business protocol. If the regulatory authorities do not expose, reprimand or fine you for these or other acts or omissions (e.g., in relation to duties or taxation) your competitors may bring your shortcomings to the attention of your potential customers or the appropriate authorities.

PARTNERSHIPS AND JOINT VENTURES

The second major option for overseas market expansion is through a partnership or joint venture (JV) agreement. The philosophy of such agreements is similar: a business arrangement mutually beneficial to both parties. It is therefore appropriate to consider them together. It is beyond the scope of this book to discuss the many types of partnership or JV arrangement available. These are adequately described in other books. We first review some advantages and disadvantages of these arrangements and then provide general and more specific advice about problem areas, in particular, potential fraud.

Many overseas business partnerships are promoted and developed through direct contact with a national resident in that country engaged in the same, or a similar type of business (possibly after an introduction effected through your embassy or the local chamber of commerce).

In other cases, joint ventures are developed to support a business arrangement between a foreign investor (business developer) and a resident 'in-country' business or enterprise. This may take the form of an input of cash and/or technology by the foreign investor. The range of partnership and joint venture agreements is very broad, and generally offers considerable advantage to both parties – especially when both businesses are involved in the same technology, or are in the same general market sector.

Advantages

The advantages for a foreign JV investor include not having to contend with major cultural differences, or to gain detailed knowledge and experience of local operating conditions, as most of these issues are usually taken care of by the local business partner. Furthermore, legal matters, licences, local rules and business protocols, language difficulties and government regulations are also usually more easily dealt with in the framework of such an arrangement.

In addition, the governments of many countries actively encourage and support JV projects by conferring special taxation benefits, easing of restrictions and regulations or the provision of Free Trade areas. They may also be prepared to underwrite the integrity of JV business arrangements to attract incoming international investment.

This is a very specialized area of market development, and is particularly suited to the manufacturing sector. If your product or process has already achieved limited and international status, you are strongly recommended to consider JV opportunities.

Disadvantages and problem areas

International business partnerships and overseas JV agreements attract international criminals such as confidence tricksters and fraudsters who are nearly always highly plausible and very experienced. The following example, which is entirely factual and in no way exaggerated, provides an indication of the risks faced by even the most experienced international business people.

■ Example

During 1996, a business acquaintance of many years' standing, highly skilled and of extensive international business experience, and very well regarded for his personal business integrity, was duped by an experienced professional criminal through a highly detailed and well-presented JV business fraud – for a total of well over US$1m.

It is not appropriate to provide the details of this case, as it is the subject of a criminal investigation and court proceedings. The personal outcome for the business man was total disaster. He lost his business, his home, his property, his convertible assets (including his motor car and pension fund), his strategic business partnerships, his business integrity and his professional reputation. He is now officially bankrupt, and in great debt. Almost all of his previous 'friends' and business acquaintances have deserted him. He is working as a poorly paid research assistant and living in poor quality rented accommodation. There is very little chance for him, at 57 years of age, to effect any form of recovery. His life is in ruins, his family in shock and despair and he has lost virtually everything he had worked for over his lifetime – including his self-confidence.

This business man – the last person we could envisage being caught in this way – was taken in by a very carefully prepared, highly organized and carefully stage managed major fraud. The criminal who perpetrated this crime is still at large and no money has been recovered. Who will he go for next?

We now provide some specific guidelines and recommendations .

Rule 1: Know who you are dealing with

The more money involved (particularly cash transfers of JV capital), usually the greater the risk. It does not matter who the potential partner is. The advice is: check them out – very, very carefully.

The first step is to commission a report from a well-established, reputable, professional international vetting organization. This usually provides a good general indication of character and basic business integrity, but this is not sufficient for evaluating a potential partner in a 'high risk' (cash-intensive) business opportunity.

You also need to obtain many references, covering many years. Do not rely on bank references alone. They are often too general. Business references, private references, particularly references from participants in previous business negotiations or projects, chambers of commerce, embassy security officers – all will help you to build a picture. Contact them all. Commission a full legal investigation itemizing court or criminal records, and a search to identify any debt problems.

Rule 2: Verify all documentation

If it is not in writing, it is worth nothing. Having thoroughly checked the character and the business history of your potential business partner, you must also check out their current businesses. If they are all registered at banks, offices or other business premises in remote, offshore locations,

257

you should be particularly careful. Although many reputable organizations are registered in such places, the fact remains that many international business frauds are perpetrated (and maintained) through remote offshore banking and 'fringe' legal representation arrangements.

Verify any documentation relating to property stated or professed to be owned by your potential business associate – both business property and private property. Ascertain who really owns it, whether it is leased, rented or even borrowed from a friend. You may find that assets are held in trust – registered to a foreign company – in the name of family members or friends.

Even when international criminals are caught, brought to court and prosecuted for theft, fraud or criminal misrepresentation, they generally have no money or assets which are recoverable against the theft or debt. They are usually adept at preventing access to their cash or convertible assets.

Rule 3: Use highly qualified, experienced professionals

Ensure that when commissioning any sort of report and when conducting any overseas business affairs, you use only the best qualified, well known and reputable internationally experienced business professionals. This advice applies also to your choice of banking and finance organizations, legal advisers, accountants and other financial advisers, contracts specialists, translators, real estate specialists and any local professional advisers.

Rule 4: Complete all checks before paying any money

Regardless of any pressure applied or opportunity presented you should never pay any money, asset or present any convertible document until you have thoroughly completed, to your own and to your professional adviser's complete satisfaction, all of the checks discussed in Rules 1–3.

Remember at all times that the larger the investment, the greater the risk. Do not take unnecessary risks in a rush to close the contract. We have never known of any partnership or JV deal which could not be delayed for a few days for additional checking to take place.

Check everything yourself and have your professionals check in great detail. Never accept any general business overview as definitive confirmation that everything is as it should be.

Despite the warnings above, remember also that all business is based upon mutual trust. The more professional you are in evaluating business opportunities and your future potential business partners, the more trusting you can become.

Political and economic instability

Pay particular attention to factors which may indicate political and/or economic instability and seek advice from your embassy, which should be well informed. In many countries (especially developing and third world countries) there are major opportunities to develop highly profitable businesses, often through JV agreements. However, such countries are often prone to political and/or economic instability, which exposes potential investors to considerable risk. In the event of a political or economic change, you may be able to rescue some of your cash assets but you may lose everything else. In general, the greater the short-term profit potential, the greater the risk. One recent example of the impact of political and economic instability is in Eastern Europe and Asia, where many much-heralded JV arrangements have foundered.

OPERATING AND LICENCE AGREEMENTS

Much of what has been said about JVs and partnerships applies also to licence agreements and operating agreements. The business arrangements between the parties in relation to licence and operating agreements are similar.

A licence (or an operating agreement) – regardless of whether it is a document required to drive a motor car, or to provide satellite television coverage across a continent – is a permission document.

Licences cause more business problems than perhaps any other type of business document. There are as many problems as there are agreements, but they may be summed up as either the licensor or licensee wishing to change some aspect of the agreement, or to do something that is not in the spirit of the agreement.

It may be that, once the licensee has taken the commercial risk and established a successful business, the licensor (perhaps a government department or regulatory body) wishes to profit excessively from that success (by, perhaps, imposing higher licence fees). Alternatively, the licensee may wish to expand the terms of the licence – to allow them to perform other functions or to secure additional geographical territory. Whatever the circumstances, often the interpretation of licence or operating agreements is subject to much disagreement, discussion, arbitration, even litigation.

The following areas in licence and operating agreements must be fully clarified.

1 **Time scales.** Check the duration (time scale) of the licence and plan accordingly. Unless you are as confident as you can be of your ROI (return on investment) over a specific period of time, and have a totally confirmed exit route, do not make large capital investments based purely upon licence availability.

2 **Renewals.** Options to renew usually cause problems. Terms such as 'On the mutual agreement of both parties' do not give an automatic right to renewal. You may be on friendly terms with the licensor, but that will not necessarily prevent them from considerably increasing the cost of the licence on renewal.

3 **Coverage.** Ensure that the geographical limits of the licence are precisely defined. The licence may state, for example, 'Within the City of . . . ' but it is necessary to ask many questions: What size is the city? How is the size defined? Who defines it? Where are the agreed boundaries? What happens if they move the city boundary? The best definition is provided by a map, but the map used must be specified precisely.

4 **Read the fine print.** Go through the licence in detail, and seek the best legal advice. Quantify, qualify, define, limit and accurately confirm, but even then there will probably be 'grey areas' open to interpretation.

5 **Find a licence expert.** Some of the best (and most experienced) experts on licence issues are employed within the television and telecommunications industry. They may not be qualified in contract law, but they do have an enormous amount of practical experience. Hire one to assist you to negotiate your licence – you will not regret it. As with business documentation, always seek the best possible professional advice.

FRANCHISE AGREEMENTS

Much of what we have said about licences and operating agreements also applies to franchise agreements.

The following general, and more specific, comments about franchises must be borne in mind if you are considering this route to export market entry.

1 **If you operate under a franchise agreement, you are responsible for your own business.** At the same time, you are subject to the franchising conditions; you are not completely your own boss, free to do whatever you like.

2 **You only get what you pay for.** Highly ethical franchise operations such as McDonald's, Pizza Hut, Ford Motor Company franchises etc. are major business opportunities. These companies have spent millions of dollars developing their businesses. They operate franchises on a global basis, they have experienced – and solved – almost every business problem associated with their franchise operations. They support their franchisees very well and provide excellent training and marketing assistance. That is why they cost a great deal of money. Do not expect to pay US$50 000 and become wealthy with an 'Uncle Bob's Car Valet Franchise'.

3 **As with JVs, there is misrepresentation and fraud at the lower end of the franchise business sector.** Problems include unfulfilled promises of franchisee support, inadequate advertising, poor training, restrictive franchisee business practices etc.

4 **Do not sign anything, do not pay a deposit, an advance or a reservation fee, do not pay for training, or even commit to long-distance travel and accommodation until you have undertaken thorough checks of the franchise operation.** You should randomly select at least four franchisees in your proposed country of operation (as listed in a telephone book), and go and visit them. Take with you all of the franchise information documentation with which you have been supplied, and identify and check all of the important points with these established franchisees. (Do not be satisfied with the comments of franchisees nominated by the franchiser.)

5 **If you are reasonably satisfied with your findings so far, make an appointment to visit the head office of the franchiser.** Do not arrange to meet at an hotel, rented office suite or similar premises.

6 **If you do decide that a franchise option is the best course of action for you to develop your market, strictly observe the franchise rules and regulations.** Otherwise you may be at risk of termination of the franchise contract, and unable to use the franchise name, provide goods or services etc. Franchisers make regular checks on franchisees and are very experienced at spotting 'irregularities' and quick to respond to infringements of the franchise agreement.

CONCLUSION

Much of this chapter concerns the pitfalls that may be experienced in undertaking an overseas business expansion and consolidation programme. Never forget that every potential business opportunity has its downside – to which you may be exposed, especially if you break the rules, even unintentionally.

We believe that, by alerting you to the potential exposures and problems of the high-risk environment of export markets, we can enable you to plan to deal with them. Regardless of how well you implement, direct, control and manage the expansion or consolidation of your overseas business, if you are unaware of the risks you may encounter, you have very little chance of recovery when you are exposed to them. 'Forearmed is forewarned', especially where major fraud is involved. Know your potential exposures. You will then greatly reduce your exposure to serious mistakes or financial penalties.

INDEX